100

THINGS TO DO IN
WASHINGTON DC
BEFORE YOU
DIE

SHANNON MORGAN

REEDY PRESS

For Steve, Finn, and Mady.
Let the adventure begin.

Library of Congress Control Number: 2014958913

ISBN: 978-1-935806-92-9

Design by Jill Halpin

Printed in the United States of America
14 15 16 17 18   5 4 3 2 1

Please note that websites, phone numbers, addresses, and company names are subject to change or cancellation. We did our best to relay the most accurate information available, but due to circumstances beyond our control, please do not hold us liable for misinformation. When exploring new destinations, please do your homework before you go.

CONTENTS

PREFACE

Washington, DC, is so much more than a political hot spot filled with memorials, monuments, and museums (although it's certainly bursting at the seams with those). It's also a hub for artists, foodies, and historians.

Arts and culture abound in Washington, DC. Whether it's the newest exhibit of modern art at the Hirshhorn, an avant-garde performance during the Capital Fringe Festival, or a classic night of jazz at the Kennedy Center, art of all kinds is celebrated throughout the city.

DC is a foodie town, too, home to food trucks and five-star restaurants alike. There are DC institutions like Ben's Chili Bowl and the Old Ebbitt Grill, as well as new-to-the-scene-but-hopefully-here-to-stay restaurants like Rose's Luxury and Le Diplomate. Restaurants open overnight, or so it seems, on 14th Street, H Street, and Barracks Row.

The city is steeped in history—and historical attractions, from the cottage where President Lincoln spent his summers during the Civil War to the grand estate of Post Cereal heiress Marjorie Merriweather Post, plus numerous sites of seminal events, like the Lincoln Memorial, where Dr. Martin Luther King Jr. delivered his famous "I Have a Dream" speech.

Washington, DC, is a four-season destination. However, certain times of the year are more visitor-friendly than are others. Hotel specials pop up whenever Congress is in recess (i.e., the whole month of August and on federal holidays). In general, weekends are more affordable than weekdays. After all, DC is a business town.

The list of attractions in this book is by no means comprehensive. It was compiled through many interviews, lots of research, and some personal experience. With few exceptions, the list is limited to District zip codes. It features both the iconic and the unique, the tried and the true, and the places we hope will stick around forever, but might not. It is accurate to the best of my knowledge at the time it was written.

This book is jam-packed with extras, but there's so much to do just outside the District that I've written a companion e-book, More Things to Do in DC. You can download it for free at ShannonMorganCreative.com.

I'd love to know what's on your DC bucket list. Please share your #100ThingsDC with me, @sldmorgan, on social media.

Happy travels!

ACKNOWLEDGMENTS

First and foremost, I'd like to thank Holly Smith. She not only opened the door to this project for me, but also applied her superb editing talents to my words.

I'd also like to thank Kate Gibbs at Destination DC for being a wealth of information.

I owe deep gratitude to the friends and strangers alike whom I interviewed for this book. Thank you for sharing what you love about Washington, DC, with me. This book belongs to you.

To my friends who cheered me on throughout the writing process, thank you!

And to my family: my husband, my children, my parents, my sister, and my in-laws, thank you for supporting me through the countless hours spent writing this book. I truly could not have finished it without you.

THINGS TO DO IN
WASHINGTON DC
BEFORE YOU

FOOD AND DRINK

BATTLE
FOR BARBECUE

Cross off the first weekend of summer. You've got plans. You'll be busy sampling some barbecue at DC's largest food and music festival.

The award-winning two-day festival pits chef against chef from the District and beyond. Backyard grill masters and celebrity chefs battle it out in several competitions, including the National Barbecue Championship, the National Pork Championship, and the Military Chef's Cook-Off. There's even a competition for America's best BBQ sauce.

Admission to the National Capital Barbecue Battle includes free food samples, cooking demos, sport exhibits, kids' activities, and concerts on three stages. Admission also includes a donation to the Capital Area Food Bank and DC's Children's Charities.

Eat up. It's a food festival you can feel good about.

National Capital Barbecue Battle
Pennsylvania Ave., between 9th & 14th Sts., NW, Washington, DC
www.bbqindc.com
Metro: Metro Center (Red, Yellow, Green lines)

EAT A HALF-SMOKE
AT BEN'S CHILI BOWL

The half-smoke, a half-pork, half-beef smoked sausage topped with chili, is the signature dish at Ben's Chili Bowl and a favorite of comedian Bill Cosby.

You can sink your teeth into this classic DC dish at a Washington Nationals game (see page 74), but you'd miss out on the experience of enjoying the dog while seated at the original counter of this fifty-five-plus-year-old establishment.

The original Ben's Chili Bowl opened in 1958 and maintains its original décor and menu. The mainstay is chili, but the menu also features burgers (veggie and beef), tuna subs and sandwiches, salads, sides, and even cake. Ben's is also open for breakfast, serving up eggs, bacon, hot cakes, and, of course, half-smokes.

Ben's Chili Bowl
1213 U St., NW, Washington, DC 20009
202-667-0909
www.benschilibowl.com
Metro: U Street (Yellow, Green lines)

HAVE DINNER
IN THE ROOF GARDEN AT ROSE'S LUXURY

Treat yourself to a one-of-a-kind experience. Book the roof garden at Rose's Luxury in Barracks Row. It's the only table where reservations are accepted at Chef Aaron Silverman's popular restaurant.

For $125 per person, you'll enjoy an all-you-can-eat (literally, your personal server will bring you food until you are full) spread of items on and off the menu. Beverages, tax, and tip are not included in the price, so you should budget a little bit more for that.

The atmosphere in the roof garden is casual and quiet. Party size is limited to ten, and there's only one seating per night. From 6:30 p.m. until close, the space is all yours.

To make a reservation, visit the Rose's Luxury website at 11 a.m. on a summer Monday. Reservations open three weeks in advance and fill up quickly. You might want to clear your calendar first. Then gather up your friends for a wonderful night of gluttony on the rooftop.

Rose's Luxury
717 8th St., SE, Washington, DC 20003
202-580-8889
www.rosesluxury.com
Metro: Eastern Market (Blue, Silver, Orange lines)

ENJOY SUNDAY BRUNCH
WITH A SHOW ON THE SIDE

Brunch is an institution in DC. It's how weekends are done. There are numerous restaurants that serve brunch in the District, but only a few offer a performance to go with your pancakes.

On Sundays, at the historic Howard Theatre, you can enjoy a southern-style buffet brunch while the Harlem Gospel Choir sings soul. The buffet features classics like fried chicken and collard greens, plus the solution for your sweet tooth, bourbon brown sugar French toast, and bottomless mimosas.

Tickets can be purchased in advance or at the door.

Howard Gospel Brunch
The Howard Theatre
620 T St., NW, Washington, DC 20001
202-803-2899
www.thehowardtheatre.com/brunch
Metro: Shaw-Howard U (Yellow, Green lines)

STUFF YOURSELF
AT TRUCKEROO

Come hungry to Truckeroo, a monthly food-truck festival held April through October. The event features more than twenty food trucks, like the Red Hook Lobster Pound truck and That Cheesecake Truck.

Grab a drink at the Bullpen, find a shady spot, and gorge on some good eats. Enjoy a variety of foods, from pizza and barbecue to crêpes and ice cream. Food trucks change from month to month, but you're still likely to find a variety of foods and cuisines.

Work off all that food with a game of cornhole, rock out to live music, and enjoy your day at the Navy Yard.

Truckeroo
Half & M Sts., SE, Washington, DC 20003
www.truckeroodc.com
Metro: Navy Yard (Green Line); Truckeroo is across the street.

Want more food trucks?
DC battles Baltimore and Philadelphia in the ultimate food-truck showdown, A Taste of Three Cities, held annually in Baltimore on the last Saturday in May.

GIVE GIN A GO
AT DC'S FIRST DISTILLERY
IN A CENTURY

"Every man has his vice." That's the motto of New Columbia Distillers, a family-run distillery, the first in the District since Prohibition.

Their artisanal spirit, Green Hat Gin, is handcrafted over a one-month period, distilled from one hundred percent grain in a copper still. The gin, with notes of citrus, coriander, and celery, is even bottled by hand. The distillery also produces a spring/summer gin, with cherry blossom and clover notes, and a barrel-aged fall/winter gin, with notes of caraway and rye.

Stop by on a Saturday afternoon for a free tasting and tour.

Green Hat Gin
New Columbia Distillers
18332 Fenwick St., NE, Washington, DC 20002
202-733-1710
www.greenhatgin.com
Metro: Rhode Island Ave.-Brentwood (Red Line)

Try a classic gin cocktail like the Rickey, the Private Eye, or the Urbanite. Recipes are available on the Green Hat Gin website.

GRAB A SLICE OF PIZZA
IN ADAMS MORGAN

DC may not be known for its pizza, but grabbing a jumbo slice after a night out in Adams Morgan is a bit of a tradition. The pizza might not be gourmet, but it'll certainly evoke memories of your college days.

There are two restaurants in Adams Morgan where you can buy a large late-night slice: Pizza Mart and Jumbo Slice Pizza. The cash-only establishments are owned by brothers who split the original business into two.

If your palate prefers another pizza, try the pies at Mellow Mushroom in Adams Morgan or one of the other places listed on page 11.

Jumbo Slice
2341 18th St., NW, Washington, DC 20009
202-234-2200

Pizza Mart
2445 18th St., NW, Washington, DC 20009
202-234-9700

Mellow Mushroom
2436 18th St., NW, Washington, DC 20009
202-290-2778
www.mellowmushroom.com/store/adams-morgan
Metro: Woodley Park/Adams Morgan (Red Line)

WHERE TO EAT PIZZA IN DC

2Amys
3715 Macomb St., NW
Washington, DC 20016
202-885-5700
www.2amyspizza.com
Metro: Cleveland Park, Van Ness (Red Line)

Comet PingPong
5037 Connecticut Ave., NW
Washington, DC 20008
202-364-0404
www.cometpingpong.com
Metro: Tenleytown-AU (Red Line)

District of Pi
910 F St., NW
Washington, DC 20004
202-393-5484
www.pi-pizza.com
Metro: Gallery Place-Chinatown or Metro
Center (Red, Yellow, Green, Orange, Silver,
Blue lines)

Etto
1541 14th St., NW
Washington, DC 20005
202-232-0920
www.ettodc.com
Metro: Gallery Place-Chinatown (Red, Yellow,
Green lines)

Fuel
1606 K St., NW
Washington, DC 20006
202-659-3835
Metro: Farragut North (Red Line)

600 F St., NW
Washington, DC 20004
202-547-3835
www.fuelpizza.com
Metro: Gallery Place-Chinatown (Red, Yellow,
Green lines)

Pizzoli's
1418 12th St., NW
Washington, DC 20005
202-234-3333
www.pizzolis.com
Metro: Mt. Vernon Square (Yellow,
Green lines)

Matchbox
713 H St., NW
Washington, DC 20001
202-289-4441
www.matchboxchinatown.com
Metro: Gallery Place-Chinatown (Red, Yellow,
Green lines)

521 8th St., SE
Washington, DC 20003
202-548-0369
www.matchboxcapitolhill.com
Metro: Eastern Market (Blue, Silver, Orange
lines)

1901 14th St., NW
Washington, DC 20009
202-328-0369
www.matchbox14thstreet.com
Metro: U Street (Yellow, Green lines)

Pizzeria Paradiso
3282 M St., NW
Washington, DC 20007
202-337-1245
Metro: Foggy Bottom (Blue, Silver, Orange
lines); transfer to Metrobus

2003 P St., NW
Washington, DC 20036
202-223-1245
www.eatyourpizza.com
Metro: Dupont Circle (Red Line)

RedRocks
1036 Park Rd., NW
Washington, DC 20010
202-506-1402
www.redrocksdc.com/
columbia-heights
Metro: Columbia Heights (Yellow,
Green lines)

1348 H St., NE
Washington, DC 20002
202-621-7300
www.redrocksdc.com/h-street
Metro: NoMa-Gallaudet (Red Line)

HAVE TEA
AT THE WILLARD

Don your designer duds and prepare your pinkie for afternoon tea at the Willard InterContinental's Peacock Alley.

A DC tradition, tea at the Willard is more than just hot drinks and finger sandwiches. It's an elegant experience set to harp music with a tea menu that mimics a wine list. Peacock Alley offers a selection of organic tea blends, from traditional English breakfast to their custom blend, Shangrila.

The prix-fixe menu includes unique sandwiches (like orange sesame chicken salad), raisin and vanilla-bean scones, and a selection of pastries that will please your sweet tooth.

Tea season begins in October and continues through the holidays, which is the ideal time to go because the Willard is all decked out for the season.

The Willard
1401 Pennsylvania Ave., NW, Washington, DC 20004
202-628-9100
www.washington.intercontinental.com
Metro: Metro Center (Red, Blue, Silver, Orange lines)

If you miss tea season,
you can enjoy it again in the spring
during the Cherry Blossom Festival.
Reservations are highly recommended, if not
essential, for any afternoon tea at the Willard.

● ●

MORE TEA, PLEASE

Tea Cellar
Park Hyatt Washington
1201 24th St., NW, Washington, DC 20037
202-789-1234
www.parkwashington.hyatt.com/en/hotel/dining/TeaCellar.html
Metro: Foggy Bottom (Blue, Silver, Orange lines)

Empress Lounge Afternoon Tea
Mandarin Oriental Washington
1300 Maryland Ave., SW, Washington, DC 20024
202-554-8588
www.mandarinoriental.com/washington/
fine-dining/empress-lounge
Metro: Smithsonian (Blue, Silver, Orange lines),
L'Enfant Plaza (Yellow, Green lines)

The Greenhouse
The Jefferson Washington DC
1200 16th St., NW, Washington, DC 20036
202-448-2300
www.jeffersondc.com/dining
Metro: Farragut North (Red Line), Farragut West
(Blue, Silver, Orange lines)

INDULGE YOUR TASTEBUDS
AT PLEASANT POPS

Cool down with a paleta, a Mexican ice pop, from Pleasant Pops. The popsicles are made from fresh, locally-sourced fruit and come in one hundred flavors. You'll have to eat yours quickly; these naturally made icy treats do not melt slowly.

You can find the Pleasant Pops truck, Big Poppa, at the Mount Pleasant farmers market on Saturdays, the Dupont Circle farmers market on Sundays, and the White House farmers market on Thursdays, April through October.

Or you can stop by the cafe any day of the year. In addition to popsicles, it serves salads, sandwiches, coffee, and tea.

Peanut Butter Nutella sandwich, anyone?

Pleasant Pops
1781 Florida Ave., NW, Washington, DC 20009
202-558-5224
www.pleasantpops.com
Metro: Dupont Circle (Red Line)

LUNCH YOUR WAY
AROUND THE WESTERN HEMISPHERE AT MITSITAM CAFE

Eat your way through five cultural regions at the Mitsitam Native Foods Cafe at the National Museum of the American Indian. The cafe celebrates the cuisines of Native Americans through five stations, each showcasing the culinary traditions of a different region through seasonal menus.

At the Northern Woodlands station, you'll find foods native to the East Coast, like maple-brined turkey and watercress salad. You'll discover salmon and bison on the menu at the Northwest Coast station, which features foods from California to Alaska. The Great Plains station offers a selection of chili and burgers to reflect a region that stretches from Texas north to Canada.

At the South American station, you'll find a variety of Brazilian and Peruvian dishes made from chicken, corn, and quinoa, and you can sample Southwestern and Mexican fare like tacos and refried black beans at the Mesoamerica station.

Mitsitam Native Foods Cafe
National Museum of the American Indian
Fourth St. & Independence Ave., SW, Washington, DC 20560
866-868-7774
www.mitsitamcafe.com
Metro: L'Enfant Plaza (Blue, Silver, Orange, Yellow, Green lines)

PAIR YOUR GRUB
WITH SUDS WHEN RESTAURANT WEEK MEETS BEER WEEK

It only happens once a year—the intersection of DC Restaurant Week and DC Beer Week. Start fasting now.

Restaurant Week occurs twice annually and is a great opportunity to try new restaurants, especially the higher-priced ones. DC Beer Week happens once a year, in August. The two events overlap by one day, when Restaurant Week ends and Beer Week begins.

Mark your calendar for the third Sunday in August. Make your reservations as soon as the participating restaurants are announced. Get your tickets to the DC Beer Week kick-off cruise. Book a pedicab for the ride home. And enjoy delicious eats paired with a sudsy pint.

DC Restaurant Week
www.ramw.org/restaurantweek

DC Beer Week
www.dcbeerweek.net

NOSH
ALONG 14TH STREET

The culinary scene on 14th Street has exploded with more than twenty-five restaurants opening up in recent years along the stretch of road between Thomas Circle and the Columbia Heights neighborhood. Here are a few to try.

Birch & Barley
1337 14th St., NW, Washington, DC 20005
202-567-2576
www.birchandbarley.com

Order one of the 555 beers on tap.

WHAT TO ORDER ON 14TH STREET

Kapnos
2201 14th St., NW
Washington, DC 20009
202-234-5000
www.kapnosdc.com
Order a Greek spread from Top Chef Mike Isabella.

Le Diplomate
1601 14th St., NW
Washington, DC 20009
202-332-3333
www.lediplomatedc.com
Order dessert and coffee; it's a French restaurant, after all!

Pearl Dive
1612 14th St., NW
Washington, DC 20009
202-319-1612
www.pearldivedc.com
Order the oysters during happy hour.

Ted's Bulletin
1818 14th St., NW
Washington, DC 20009
202-265-8337
www.tedsbulletin14thstreet.com
Order the homemade pop tarts.

ORDER RAMEN
AT DAIKAYA IN CHINATOWN

Give ramen a second chance at Daikaya in Chinatown. It's not the cheap stuff you remember from your college days. It is a delicious noodle soup that has become a cuisine all its own in DC.

Daikaya serves Sapporo-style ramen made with Japanese noodles. There's even a vegan ramen on the menu.

Daikaya is actually two separate restaurants under one roof. The first floor is a traditional ramen shop. It's bright and busy, meant to serve up soup in a hurry. Upstairs is the izakaya, or sake shop. It serves Japanese comfort foods in a casual, bar-like setting that invites diners to relax against the warm wood tones of the bar and linger awhile.

Daikaya
705 6th St., NW, Washington, DC 20001
202-589-1600
www.daikaya.com
Metro: Gallery Place-Chinatown (Red, Yellow, Green lines)

Book a table in February and enjoy the Chinese New Year Festival, too. While you're in Chinatown, check out the Friendship Archway. You can't miss it.

RAMEN ON THE RED LINE

Nooshi
1120 19th St., NW, Washington, DC 20036
202-293-3138
www.nooshidc.com
Metro: Farragut North (Red Line)

Sakuramen
2441 18th St., NW, Washington, DC 20009
202-656-5285
www.sakuramen.info
Metro: Adams Morgan-Woodley Park-Zoo (Red Line)

Toki Underground
1234 H St., NE, Washington, DC 20002
202-388-3086
www.tokiunderground.com
Metro: NoMa-Gallaudet (Red Line)

RAISE YOUR GLASS
AT THE BAR WITH
THE BEST VIEW IN DC

Dress up for drinks at POV, the sophisticated rooftop bar at the W Hotel. From the open-air lounge you can see many of DC's iconic landmarks. The view is stunning during the day, but spectacular at night when the monuments are illuminated.

The bar is designed to celebrate these views, with a White House Corner on the north side and a Washington Monument Corner southside. However, the most stunning feature might just be on the inside, a fifty-foot red-tape wall sculpture that's a nod to Washington bureaucracy. The indoor lounge also features presidential profiles made of glowing brass pegs.

Seating is first come, first serve. Come dressed to impress and order a drink that captures Washington, DC, in a glass.

POV Lounge at the W Hotel
515 15th St., NW, Washington, DC 20004
202-661-2400
www.wwashingtondc.com/pov
Metro: Metro Center (Red Line)

CHEERS!

Order a classic cocktail at the Rye Bar in the ultra-luxurious Capella Hotel in Georgetown. American rye whiskey is tapped from a barrel behind the bar and poured over hand-shaved, pure-water ice cubes.

The Rye Bar at Capella
1050 31st St., NW, Washington, DC 20007
202-617-2425
www.thegrillroomdc.com/the-rye-bar/
upscale-bars-georgetown

Metro: Foggy Bottom (Blue, Silver,
Orange lines); transfer to a
Metrobus to Georgetown

RESERVE A SEAT
AT MINIBAR BY JOSÉ ANDRÉS

One of the hottest places to eat in DC is minibar by José Andrés, if only because reservations are so elusive. Reservations are accepted only by e-mail and only seasonally: December 1 for January-March; March 1 for April-June; June 1 for July-September; and September 1 for October-December. In addition, there are only four seatings of just six per night.

At $250 per person, dinner at minibar truly is a special occasion, and Chef Andrés does not disappoint. He serves up an innovative tasting menu that will tease your taste buds and give you a culinary experience like no other.

minibar by José Andrés
855 E St., NW, Washington, DC 20004
202-393-0812
www.minibarbyjoseandres.com
Metro: Gallery Place-Chinatown (Red, Yellow, Green lines),
Archives-Navy Memorial (Yellow, Green lines)

> **Grab a cocktail at barmini,
> next door, before dinner.**

NO RESERVATIONS

Can't get a reservation at minibar?
Try one of these José Andrés
restaurants instead.

Jaleo
480 7th St., NW, Washington, DC 20004
202-628-7949
www.jaleo.com/dc
Metro: Archives-Navy Memorial (Yellow, Green lines)

Oyamel
401 7th St., NW, Washington, DC 20004
202-628-1005
www.oyamel.com
Metro: Archives-Navy Memorial (Yellow, Green lines)

Zaytinya
701 9th St., NW, Washington, DC 20001
202-638-0800
www.zaytinya.com
Metro: Gallery Place-Chinatown (Red, Yellow, Green lines)

RUB ELBOWS
WITH POLITICOS AT THE OLD EBBITT GRILL

Step back in time at the oldest saloon in Washington, DC, the Old Ebbitt Grill. Slide into one of the mahogany and velvet booths, or belly up to the marble and brass bar, and you just might rub elbows with a politician. This watering hole has been a favorite of presidents and politicos since it first opened in 1856. The Beaux-Arts-style décor echoes the original design of the saloon and features a few original relics, like an antique clock, beer steins, and a walrus head courtesy of President Theodore Roosevelt.

Best known for its raw bar and five varieties of oysters, the Old Ebbitt Grill also serves a mean burger. Pair your meal with a glass of wine or a pint of beer from their extensive drink menu.

Old Ebbitt Grill
675 15th St., NW, Washington, DC 20005
202-347-4800
www.ebbitt.com
Metro: Metro Center (Red, Blue, Silver, Orange lines)

GO OFF THE RECORD

Another bar where you can enjoy a power lunch alongside the Washington elite is at the Hay-Adams Hotel. Check out the political caricatures while you're there.

Off the Record
800 16th St., NW, Washington, DC 20006
202-942-7599
www.hayadams.com/washington-dc-bars
Metro: McPherson Square
(Blue, Silver, Orange lines)

SHOP
THE MARKETS

Shopping the open-air markets is a DC tradition, especially on the weekends when the markets are more than just a line of vendor stalls. They serve as a community hub, featuring live entertainment and local art alongside fresh produce and baked goods. Many, like Eastern Market, have been in operation for more than a hundred years. Others, like the FRESHFARM markets, are newer but just as loved.

DC MARKETS

Eastern Market
Tuesday-Sunday
225 7th St., SE
Washington, DC 20003
202-698-5253
www.easternmarket-dc.org
Metro: Eastern Market (Blue, Silver, Orange lines)

FRESHFARM Markets
CityCenter DC, Dupont Circle,
Foggy Bottom, H Street, Mount Vernon
Triangle, Penn Quarter, Union Market, White House
www.freshfarmmarkets.org

Georgetown Flea Market
Sundays
1819 35th St., NW
Washington, DC 20007
202-775-3532
www.georgetownfleamarket.com
Metro: Foggy Bottom (Blue, Silver, Orange lines);
transfer to Metrobus

Maine Avenue Fish Market
Open daily; largest selection Fridays-Sunday
Maine Ave. & Water St., SW
Washington, DC 20024
Metro: L'Enfant Plaza
(Blue, Silver, Orange, Yellow, Green lines)

Union Market
Tuesday-Sunday
1309 5th St., NE
Washington, DC 20002
301-652-7400
www.unionmarketdc.com
Metro: NoMa-Gallaudet (Red Line)

WINE & DINE YOUR SWEETHEART
DURING DATE NIGHT DC

You can woo your sweetheart any time of year, but in February, you can save some money while you do it during Date Night DC, when many restaurants entice couples with delicious promotions. Combine dinner with an attraction and you've got a fun night out on the town.

Here are a few ideas:

- Go out for pizza (see pages 10-11), and then take in a show at the Atlas (see page 43).
- Have a picnic dinner by the Reflecting Pool, then take a pedicab (see page 52), or moonlight tour of the memorials (see page 110).
- Take a dinner cruise on the Potomac (see page 120).
- Enjoy cocktails at POV (see page 22), and then a performance on Millennium Stage (see page 40).

For more date-night ideas, visit www.washington.org/100-date-ideas.

MUSIC AND ENTERTAINMENT

ATTEND THE
FORT RENO PARK
SUMMER CONCERT SERIES

Spend your summer weeknights listening to music and enjoying the view at Fort Reno Park. Fort Reno was built in 1861 at the highest point in DC to defend the city during the Civil War. It was the largest fort in the city. Today, it functions as a park, reservoir, and concert venue.

On Mondays and Thursdays, up-and-coming DC-area musicians share their sounds with the families in attendance. The concerts are free and very family-friendly; no alcohol is allowed. Three bands typically play from 7 to 9:30 p.m.

Fort Reno Park
Chesapeake St. & Nebraska Ave., NW, Washington, DC 20016
202-355-6356
www.fortreno.com
www.nps.gov/cwdw/historyculture/fort-reno.htm
Metro: Tenleytown (Red Line)

> **If you enjoyed the show, consider making a donation to the Washington Peace Center, the fiscal sponsor of the concert series The series is run entirely by volunteers; donations are appreciated to keep it going.**

GATHER IN
DUPONT CIRCLE
FOR THE ANNUAL HIGH HEEL RACE

Get your camera and costume ready for a DC Halloween tradition, the annual High Heel Race in Dupont Circle. On the Tuesday before Halloween, men dress up in drag and race down 17th Street in heels—all for beer.

This informal block party draws more spectators than participants and attracts a diverse crowd. The crowd gathers around 6 p.m., although the actual race doesn't happen until 9 p.m. Dupont Circle restaurants and bars offer specials to celebrate the annual event.

It's all in good fun. Bring your sense of humor and pose for a picture with a costumed "lady."

17th Street High Heel Race
17th St. between P & S Sts., NW, Washington, DC 20036
www.facebook.com/pages/17th-Street-High-Heel-Race/293167114030193
Metro: Dupont Circle (Red Line)

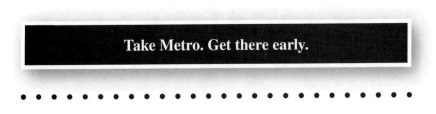

Take Metro. Get there early.

DISCOVER
ELLINGTON'S DC

Jazz great Duke Ellington was born and raised in Washington, DC. Here are a few spots around his former U Street stomping grounds that jazz fans will enjoy seeing.

Bohemian Caverns Jazz Club
2001 11th St., NW, Washington, DC 20001
202-299-0800
www.bohemiancaverns.com
Metro: Shaw-Howard U (Yellow, Green lines)

Duke Ellington Birthplace & Mural by Aniekan Udofia
The Duke Ellington Building (Post Office)
2121 Ward Ct., NW, Washington, DC 20037
Metro: Dupont Circle (Red Line)

Duke Ellington Mural by G. Byron Peck
True Reformer Building
1200 U St., NW, Washington, DC 20009
Metro: U Street (Yellow, Green lines)

Lincoln Theatre
1215 U St., NW, Washington, DC 20009
202-888-0050
www.thelincolndc.com
Metro: U Street (Yellow, Green lines)

ALL THAT JAZZ

DC is a jazzy city. Get your fix at these venues and events.

Blues Alley

1073 Wisconsin Ave., NW, Washington, DC 20007
202-337-4141
www.bluesalley.com
Metro: Foggy Bottom (Blue, Silver, Orange lines); transfer to Metrobus

DC Jazz Festival in June

www.dcjazzfest.org

HR-57

www.hr57.org

Jazz in the Garden

Summer Fridays 5-8:30 p.m.
National Gallery of Art Sculpture Garden
(see page 64)

Jazz Night in Southwest

Fridays 6-9 p.m.
Westminster Presbyterian Church
400 I St., SW, Washington, DC 20024
202-484-7700
www.westminsterdc.org/jazz-night-in-dc
Metro: Waterfront (Green Line)

KC Jazz Club

Kennedy Center
www.kennedy-center.org/programs/jazz/jazzclub
(see page 40)

Take 5

Third Thursday
Luce Foundation Center for American Art
(see page 37)

SALUTE THE MARINES
AT 8TH & I

On Friday evenings in summer, you can witness a ceremony held at the oldest active post in the Marine Corps, the Marine Barracks Washington, DC. The ceremony begins at 8:45 p.m. with a concert by the US Marine Band and is followed by the Evening Parade.

Reservations, which can be made online, are recommended to secure a seat at the parade. You should arrive between 7 p.m. and 8 p.m. to claim your seat, or it may be given away to those waiting without tickets. There's no parking at the barracks, but there is a free shuttle from Maritime Plaza if you opt to park there.

Locally known as "8th & I" as a nod to its location, the Marine Barracks Washington, DC, was founded by President Thomas Jefferson and Lt. Col. William Ward Burrows in 1801.

Semper Fidelis. Oorah!

Marine Barracks Washington, DC
8th & I Sts., SE, Washington, DC 20390
www.barracks.marines.mil/Parades/GeneralInformation.aspx
Metro: Eastern Market (Blue, Silver, Orange lines)

HAVE COFFEE AND JAM
WITH THE ARTISTS AT THE LUCE

Grab yourself some free coffee (or tea) weekend afternoons from 1:30-3:30 p.m. at the Luce Foundation Center when the Smithsonian American Art Museum hosts Art + Coffee, talks with local artists.

Alternatively, make plans to visit the Luce for its monthly concert series, Luce Unplugged. This event features an artwork talk followed by a live acoustic performance inspired by the art.

Both of these events are part of the Luce Local Artist series. The Luce also offers a drawing class on Tuesdays. The Luce Foundation Center for American Art is an art-storage and study center that features 3,000 works of art on three levels for public view. It's an interactive and innovative experience of American art.

Luce Foundation Center for American Art
Smithsonian American Art Museum
8th and F Sts., NW, Washington, DC 20004
202-633-7970
www.americanart.si.edu/luce/index.cfm
Metro: Gallery Place-Chinatown (Red, Yellow, Green lines)

Before you go, download one of six scavenger hunts online at the Luce and have fun solving it during your visit.

WATCH A MOVIE
ON THE GREEN

Grab a blanket and some popcorn and enjoy a free movie under the stars. Here are several outdoor spots where you can watch a movie on the green from late spring to early fall in DC. Dates and showtimes vary by location.

Adams Morgan Movie Night
2201 18th St., NW, Washington, DC 20009
www.adamsmorganmovienights.com
Metro: Dupont Circle (Red Line)

Canal Park Movies
202 M St., SE, Washington, DC 20003
www.canalparkdc.org
Metro: Navy Yard (Green Line)

Cinemas in the Circle
Dupont Circle
www.dupontfestival.com
Metro: Dupont Circle (Red Line)

Gateway DC Summer Film Series
2700 Martin Luther King Ave., SE, Washington, DC 20032
www.gatewaydcfilms.com
Metro: Congress Heights (Green Line)

Golden Cinema Series
Farragut Square: Connecticut Ave. & K St., NW, Washington, DC 20036
www.goldentriangledc.com/do/golden-cinema-series1
Metro: Farragut North (Red Line)

NoMa Summer Screen
Second & L Sts., NE, Washington, DC 20002
www.nomabid.org/noma-summer-screen
Metro: NoMa-Gallaudet (Red Line)

Screens on the Green at the National Mall
7th & 12th Sts., SW, Washington, DC 20024
www.friendsofscreenonthegreen.org
Metro: L'Enfant Plaza (Yellow, Green, Blue, Silver, Orange lines)

Union Market Drive-In
1309 5th St., NE, Washington, DC 20002
www.unionmarketdc.com/events
Metro: NoMa-Gallaudet (Red Line)

For the complete schedule, visit DC Outdoor Films online at
www.dcoutdoorfilms.com.

GET REEL: DC FILM FESTIVALS

DC Environmental Film
Festival, March
www.dcenvironmentalfilmfest.org

DC Shorts Film Festival,
November
www.dcshorts.com

Reel Affirmations, November
www.reelaffirmations.org

Washington DC International
Film Festival, April
www.filmfestdc.org

ENJOY A FREE PERFORMANCE
ON MILLENNIUM STAGE

Walk into the Kennedy Center and you'll notice a stage set up on the north side of the Grand Foyer. This is the Millennium Stage, an intimate stage set a few red-carpeted steps down into an expansive hallway. Here, musicians, singers, dancers, actors, and other artists perform every night.

For free.

That's right, free. No tickets required. Just come and enjoy the performance. Shows are held at 6 p.m. every evening. In addition, Millennium Stage presents the Conservatory Project, a showcase of exceptional young artists, in February and May.

Millennium Stage was created in response to Performing Arts for Everyone, an initiative that strives to make the arts accessible. The daily free performances make the Kennedy Center, a living memorial to President John F. Kennedy Jr., accessible to all.

Millennium Stage
The John F. Kennedy Center for the Performing Arts
2700 F St., NW, Washington, DC 20566
202-467-4600
www.kennedy-center.org/programs/millennium/schedule.html
Metro: Foggy Bottom-GWU (Blue, Silver, Orange lines)

TIP

When you go, be sure
to visit the roof terrace.
It wraps around the building
and provides a stunning view
of the city. Stop by the
Roof Terrace Restaurant
for dinner or brunch.

GET TICKETS
TO THE AMERICAN THEATER

There are plenty of great theater companies in the District, but if you want to see a show by an American playwright, then you must get tickets to Arena Stage. Founded in 1950, Arena Stage is dedicated to telling American stories created by American artists. Today, it's a national center for American theater.

In its home at the Mead Center, three venues comprise Arena Stage: a 680-seat four-sided theater for shows in-the-round; a 514-seat historic theater with a proscenium arch; and a 200-seat theater for new, innovative performances. In all, Arena Stage is the largest performing arts center in DC after the Kennedy Center.

Shows include comedies, dramas, political satires, and more—anything by an American playwright or about American culture—from yesterday, today, and tomorrow.

Arena Stage
1101 6th St., SW, Washington, DC 20024
202-554-9066
www.arenastage.org
Metro: Waterfront-SEU (Green Line)

GO
TO THE ATLAS

You can't miss the Atlas Theater when you visit H Street. Its historic marquee, reminiscent of early Hollywood, beckons theatergoers with white and blue lights.

The theater first opened in 1938, showing *Love Finds Andy Hardy* starring Mickey Rooney. Today, it is the cornerstone of the H Street arts and entertainment district and a hub for the performing arts.

More than just a performance venue, the Atlas fosters collaborative art, offering rehearsal space and education to actors, dancers, and musicians alike.

The Atlas features five stages on which a variety of performances are set. You can expect to see everything from comedy acts to operettas. The Atlas Intersections Festival, an all-arts showcase that runs in February and March, is a great opportunity to experience the venue.

Atlas Performing Arts Center
1333 H St., NE, Washington, DC 20002
202-399-7993
www.atlasarts.org
Metro: Union Station (Red Line)

• •

CELEBRATE THE HOLIDAY SEASON
IN THE DISTRICT

December is a beautiful time of year to visit Washington, DC. Yes, it's cold, but the holiday spirit will keep you warm. Here are just some of the ways DC celebrates the season.

Christmas at the Willard
Thanksgiving–December 30
www.washington.intercontinental.com/holiday-events

Brunch, tea, caroling, and decked halls. See page 12 for more about the Willard.

Downtown Holiday Market
Thanksgiving–December 23
8th & F Sts., NW
Washington, DC 20004
www.downtownholidaymarket.com
Metro: Gallery Place-Chinatown (Red, Yellow, Green lines)

Shop the market for that one-of-a-kind artisan gift.

ZooLights
Thanksgiving–January 1
www.nationalzoo.si.edu/activitiesandevents/celebrations/zoolights

See the National Zoo illuminated by more than 500,000 LED lights. See page 48 for more about the National Zoo.

National Chanukah Menorah
The White House Ellipse
E & 15th Sts., NW
Washington, DC 20500
www.nationalmenorah.org
Metro: Federal Triangle, McPherson Square (Blue, Silver, Orange lines), Metro Center (Red, Blue, Silver, Orange lines)

Tickets to the lighting ceremony are required, but are free and available online.

National Christmas Tree Lighting
The White House Ellipse
E & 15th Sts., NW
Washington, DC 20500
www.thenationaltree.org
Metro: Federal Triangle, McPherson Square (Blue, Silver, Orange lines), Metro Center (Red, Blue, Silver, Orange lines)

The lottery for the ceremony opens in October. The tree is illuminated through January 1.

WATCH THE
ELEPHANTS ON PARADE

They may not be pink like the elephants in the Disney classic Dumbo, but these pachyderms do parade when they arrive in DC in March. When the Barnum & Bailey Circus comes to town, the elephants walk in line to the Verizon Center accompanied by acrobats and clowns.

The evening event begins near Garfield Park and follows Washington Avenue north to 3rd Street before turning toward the Verizon Center. Third Street provides the best viewing spots.

Take the Blue, Silver, or Orange lines to the Capitol South Metro stop to see the start of the parade, or take the Red, Yellow, or Green lines to Gallery Place to reach the end of the parade route. Follow @DCElephantWalk on Twitter for updates on the event.

PARTY
ON H STREET

Like street fairs? In DC, the H Street Festival is one of the best. This September tradition is ten blocks of food, fun, and community. The event features artisans and community organizations, neighborhood restaurants and shops, and loads of performers on several stages. From jazz and gospel to pop and interpretative art, the entertainment options are plentiful.

Come hungry and bring your steel stomach for the annual pie-, chili-, or burrito-eating contests, or just nosh your way from food truck to food truck. Work your biceps in the arm-wrestling competition. Ride along H Street in a pedicab or on the DC Streetcar. Let the kids go wild on the giant inflatables and enjoy an afternoon of fun on H Street.

H Street Festival
400-1400 blocks
www.hstreet.org/events/festival
Metro: Union Station (Red Line)

Another great neighborhood festival is Adams Morgan Day, also in September. www.adamsmorgandayfest.com

SPORTS AND RECREATION

SEE THE GIANT
PANDAS

Travel the Asian Trail at the National Zoo to the Panda House to catch a glimpse of a giant panda, one of the rarest animals in the world. The National Zoo is home to three: Mei Xiang, Tian Tian, and their cub, Bao Bao.

The indoor and outdoor exhibit mimics the pandas' habitat in China and features the experience zone, where you can cool down like a panda and get a close-up look at the pandas through a glass divider.

Extremely popular, the panda exhibit is best visited in the morning. However, a morning visit doesn't guarantee a panda sighting. If the gentle giants are elusive on your visit, you may have to watch for them via the free online panda cam instead.

National Zoo
3001 Connecticut Ave., NW, Washington, DC 20008
202-633-4888
www.nationalzoo.si.edu
Metro: Woodley Park-Adams Morgan (Red Line)

The giant pandas will likely return to China in the next few years. Go see them before they're gone.

ZOO-RIFIC EVENTS

Mark your calendar for these annual
events at the National Zoo:

Easter Monday, Spring
Kids' Farm Month, April
ZooFari, May
Brew at the Zoo, July
Animals in the Sky, July
Bao Bao's Birthday, August
Rock-N-Roar, September
Zoo Fiesta, September
Autumn Conservation Festival, October
Boo at the Zoo, October
Night of the Living Zoo, October
ZooLights, Thanksgiving through New Year's Day

SEE THE
SMITHSONIAN BY SEGWAY

See the city by Segway; the Smithsonian Tour is the only one of its kind that departs from the National Mall. Segway leads three tours daily, each three hours in length.

The tour begins with a Segway orientation and safety video. Then riders set out from the National Museum of American History to explore the National Mall, visiting many of the Smithsonian museums and gardens and sharing their stories.

You'll also glide by many of Washington's famous landmarks, monuments, and memorials as you cover more than five miles and 1,000 acres, learning fun facts about the city along the way.

Smithsonian Tours by Segway
Kiosk in front of the National Museum of American History
1400 Constitution Ave., NW, Washington, DC 20560
202-384-8516
www.segway.com/SmithsonianTours
Metro: Smithsonian, Federal Triangle (Blue, Silver, Orange lines)

You must be at least 16 years old and weigh between 100 and 260 pounds to ride a Segway. Tours are popular, so book yours early.

SMITHSONIAN CELEBRATIONS

Mark your calendar for these annual
Smithsonian events.

Smithsonian Craft Show, April

National Building Museum, Great Hall

401 F St., NW, Washington, DC 20001

www.smithsoniancraftshow.org

Metro: Judiciary Square (Red Line)

Smithsonian Folklife Festival

Last week of June & first week of July

National Mall

www.festival.si.edu

Metro: Smithsonian (Blue, Silver, Orange lines)

Smithsonian Heritage Months Celebrations

Black History Month, February

Women's History Month, March

Asian Pacific Heritage Month, May

Hispanic Heritage Month, September 15-October 15

American Indian Heritage Month, November

www.smithsonianeducation.org/heritage_month/
bhm/index.html

HAIL A PEDICAB

Skip the taxi and hail a pedicab—a two-seat cart pulled by a bicycle—instead. Pedicabs are just like taxis. Drivers wheel their passengers around the city, picking up baseball fans after a Washington Nationals game or driving home couples after date night in Georgetown.

Pedicabs are also used for weddings, special events, and tours of the city. Capitol Pedicabs offers tours of the Washington Monument and the Jefferson, FDR, Korean War, Lincoln, World War II, and Vietnam Veterans memorials. DC Pedicab offers sightseeing tours of the National Mall, Capitol Hill, and Embassy Row. National Pedicabs pedals passengers around the east side of the National Mall and by the monuments and memorials.

All offer custom tour packages so you can see the city your way: from the backseat.

Capitol Pedicabs
202-232-6085
www.capitolpedicabs.com

DC Pedicab
202-345-8065
www.dcpedicab.com

National Pedicabs
202-269-9090
www.nationalpedicabs.com

WATCH THE PLANES
AND PLAY IN THE SAND AT HAINS POINT

Grab the kids (or kids at heart) and head to the Hains Point picnic area. Here you'll find a playground where the kiddos can climb, play in the sand, and watch the planes from Reagan National Airport.

Hains Point is at the tip of East Potomac Park, which extends south from the Thomas Jefferson Memorial. The peninsula is flanked by the Potomac River and the Washington Channel, so it's a great place to get near (but not in) the water, too.

East Potomac Park is also home to public golf courses, a tennis center, and a swimming pool. In the spring, the park is abloom with cherry blossoms (see page 67), and, in October, sees runners in the Marine Corps Marathon along its trails.

Hains Point at East Potomac Park
900 Ohio Dr., SW, Washington, DC 20024
202-426-6841
www.nps.gov/nama/planyourvisit/outdooractivities.htm
Metro: Smithsonian (Blue, Silver, Orange lines); walk from the
Thomas Jefferson Memorial. There is parking along Ohio Drive
if you arrive by car instead.

PICNIC IN A
GROVE OF STATE TREES

Where can you picnic in a grove of trees from every state in the Union? At the United States National Arboretum.

The thirty-acre National Grove of State Trees is home to the official state trees from all fifty states and the District of Columbia. Each one is identified by a metal sign. Picnic tables are located near the entrance; it's the only picnic spot inside the arboretum.

The arboretum is also home to the National Bonsai & Penjing Museum, the Capitol Columns, and numerous collections of plants and flowers. During the spring and fall, you can tour the arboretum on an open-air tram. The thirty-five-minute narrated tour explains the history of the arboretum and covers most of its 446 acres.

The United States National Arboretum
3501 New York Ave., NE, Washington, DC 20002
202-245-2726
www.usna.usda.gov
Metro: Stadium Armory (Blue, Silver, Orange lines);
transfer to the B2 Metrobus

> **Plan your visit for a weekend. The Arboretum is closed Tuesdays–Thursdays.**

HOW DOES YOUR GARDEN GROW?

Aquatic Gardens at Kenilworth Park
1550 Anacostia Ave., NE, Washington, DC 20019
202-426-6905
www.nps.gov/keaq
Metro: Deanwood (Orange Line)

Smithsonian Gardens
National Mall
www.gardens.si.edu

United States Botanic Gardens
100 Maryland Ave., SW, Washington, DC 20001
202-225-8333
www.usbg.gov
Metro: Federal Center (Blue, Silver, Orange lines)

ASCEND
THE EXORCIST STEPS

Tucked between an ivy-covered stone wall and a red brick building in Georgetown is a steep, narrow, multi-level staircase that rises from Canal Road to Prospect Street. The stairwell was made famous by the final scene in *The Exorcist* when Father Karas is thrown out of a window, tumbling down the stairs to his death.

At night, the stairwell glows red from the streetlights bouncing off the brick. At the top is the house where possessed protagonist Regan MacNeil lived in the movie. There's a black fence in front to keep fans out.

You'll find the Exorcist Steps by taking 36th Street to M Street and going around the left side of the building at 3600 M Street. The stairs stand where M Street becomes Canal Road.

Just don't fall (or talk to any demons) on your way up.

Exorcist Steps
3600 M St., NW, Washington, DC 20007
maps.georgetown.edu/exorciststeps
Metro: Foggy Bottom-GWU (Blue, Silver, Orange lines);
transfer to Metrobus

**Avoid the steps on the weekends if you want
a good photo opp. They're popular with runners
and other fitness fiends.**

A SECRET GARDEN IN THE CITY

Stroll through the side streets of Dupont Circle to reach the Spanish steps, a hidden staircase that ascends both sides of a lion head fountain, and enjoy the park-like setting in the middle of a bustling neighborhood.

The Spanish Steps
22nd & Decatur Sts., NW, Washington, DC 20008
Metro: Dupont Circle (Red Line)

RIDE YOUR BIKE
TO ALL 50 STATES (AVENUES, THAT IS)

Mark your calendar for September and prepare to register early for the popular 50 States Ride. The annual bike ride travels sixty-two miles through all eight wards of the District along all fifty state avenues.

The event begins at 8 a.m. with check-in the hour before. The exact location of check-in is emailed the week before the event, and the actual route is kept secret until the day of the ride. Don't worry, there are route marshals on hand should you get lost. There are also four predetermined pit stops on the route where you can catch up.

Not up for the sixty-two-mile 50 States Ride? Sign up for the shorter fifteen-mile 13 Colonies Ride instead. It loops through Northeast and Southeast Washington with one pit stop along the way. Both rides end in the same location, with a post-ride celebration from 2-6 p.m.

50 States & 13 Colonies Ride
Washington Area Bike Association
www.waba.org/50-states-13-colonies

Need a bike? Check out Capital Bikeshare.
And don't forget your helmet!
www.capitalbikeshare.com

BIKE
THE BOUNDARY

Another option for serious bikers is the Boundary Stones Ride, also in September but less formal than the 50 States & 13 Colonies Ride.

If you look at a map of Washington, DC, the boundary lines form a diamond. The actual boundaries are marked by forty stones along the sixty-two-mile perimeter.

The Boundary Stones Ride sets out to bike each side of the perimeter, from stone to stone. You can ride just one side or all four, whatever works for you. Meet at the designated point at 9:30 a.m. and ride through the afternoon.

DC Boundary Stones
www.boundarystones.org
Bike route: www.bikely.com/maps/
bike-path/boundary-stone-bike-ride

> **With a little planning, you can bike the boundary stones and the fifty state avenues on your own. Just bring a buddy who is up to the challenge, too.**

WALK
THE NEIGHBORHOOD HERITAGE TRAILS

Walk through history when you follow the Neighborhood Heritage Trails. Each trail tells the story of the neighborhood through photos, maps, and destination points. Along the way, you'll discover the shops, restaurants, and residents that make each neighborhood unique.

The trails explore several neighborhoods throughout the District: Adams Morgan, Barracks Row, Brightwood, Columbia Heights, Deanwood, Downtown, Federal Triangle, Georgia Ave./ Pleasant Plains, H Street, Logan Circle, Mount Pleasant, Shaw, Southwest, Tenleytown, and U Street. There's also an African American Heritage Trail that spans several neighborhoods.

Maps are available on the Cultural Tourism DC website. The Downtown and U Street trails even have mobile apps and audio tours.

What are you waiting for? Download the maps and booklets and hit the trails.

Neighborhood Heritage Trails
Cultural Tourism DC
www.culturaltourismdc.org/portal/neighborhood-heritage-trails

ESCAPE
TO THE PRESIDENTIAL FOREST

Go on an island safari off the coast of the capital. Take a ranger-led walking tour of Roosevelt Island, the living memorial to President Theodore Roosevelt. It celebrates Roosevelt's love of the outdoors—which is reflected in quotes posted around the island—and is a favorite of outdoor enthusiasts.

This presidential forest is an escape from the urban jungle of the District. It features the flat Swamp Trail and boardwalk and the gravelly Woods and Upland trails, as well as a connecting trail to both the eighteen-mile Mount Vernon Trail and a ten-mile segment of the Potomac Heritage Trail.

When you visit, expect to see runners on the trails, bird-watchers in the woods, and kayakers and canoers on the Potomac. There's no camping on the island.

Theodore Roosevelt Island
www.nps.gov/this/index.htm
Metro: Rosslyn (Blue, Silver, Orange lines),
walk toward the Key Bridge and follow the trail to the island,
a ten-minute walk away

Use caution when visiting the island in the winter months. The trails can be slippery.

GO ROLLER SKATING
IN ANACOSTIA PARK

When was the last time you went roller skating? Roller rinks are few and far between in the District, but you can lace up your skates at Anacostia Park in southeast DC. The skating pavilion is covered, and skate rentals are free. Take a few spins around the rink, then enjoy the other amenities at the park, like the eighteen-hole golf course and basketball court. You can also go canoeing and fishing or watch for bald eagles from the sea wall.

While you're in Anacostia, visit the Frederick Douglass National Historical Site (see page 134), and the Kenilworth Aquatic Gardens (see page 55), an all-seasons outdoor nature center great for exploring ponds and watching birds.

Skating Pavilion at Anacostia Park
1900 Anacostia Dr., SE, Washington, DC 20020
202-472-3884
www.nps.gov/anac/planyourvisit/things2do.htm
Metro: Anacostia (Green Line)

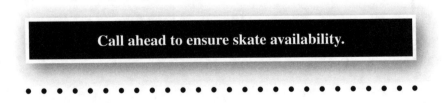

Call ahead to ensure skate availability.

GET BACK TO NATURE
AT ROCK CREEK PARK

Start your visit to one of DC's largest parks at the Nature Center. Here you can see turtles and snakes, watch for birds from the observation deck, or go for a hike on the Woodland Trail. You can also take a look at the night sky at the planetarium.

Another must-do on your Rock Creek bucket list—horseback riding. From spring to fall, you can take an hour-long, guided trail ride from the Rock Creek Park Horse Center. No experience is necessary, and the ride travels at a walking pace.

Rock Creek is more than just nature walks and trail rides, though. Near 16th Street, you'll discover the Carter Barron Amphitheater, home to a summer concert series, and on Tilden Street, the Peirce Mill, an operational grist mill that dates back to the eighteen hundreds.

Rock Creek Park Nature Center and Planetarium
5200 Glover Rd., NW, Washington, DC 20015
www.nps.gov/rocr
Metro: Friendship Heights (Red Line)

Rock Creek Park Horse Center
5100 Glover Rd., NW
Washington, DC 20015
202-362-0117
www.rockcreekhorsecenter.com

Peirce Mill and Barn
2401 Tilden St., NW
Washington, DC 20015
Metro: Van Ness (Red Line)

GO ICE SKATING
IN A SCULPTURE GARDEN

Lace up your skates and slide by the sculpture garden at the National Gallery of Art. Skate to music by daylight or under the twinkle of white lights and stars. If you're a novice, don't worry, guest services has you covered. They offer group and private lessons for kids, adults, and even hockey enthusiasts and provide skate rentals for a nominal fee.

After your two-hour session, warm up with a cup of soup or hot cocoa at the Pavilion Cafe. Or cozy up with beer, wine, or sangria. Just save the drinking for after the skating.

National Gallery of Art Sculpture Garden Ice Rink
7th St. & Constitution Ave., NW, Washington, DC 20565
202-216-9397
www.nga.gov/content/ngaweb/visit/ice-rink.html
Open mid-November to mid-March
Metro: Archives (Yellow, Green lines)

The ice rink is open long after the museum closes for the night. During evening hours, access the rink from its 9th Street entrance.

DC ON ICE

Washington Harbour Ice Rink
3000 K St., NW, Washington, DC 20007
202-706-7666
www.thewashingtonharbour.com/skating
Metro: Foggy Bottom (Blue, Silver, Orange lines);
transfer to Metrobus

Canal Park Ice Rink
200 M St., SE, Washington, DC 20003
www.canalparkdc.org/ice-rink
Metro: Navy Yard (Green Line)

RIDE THE
ONE-OF-A-KIND CAROUSEL

Be a kid again. Take a ride on the National Carousel. The carousel was built in 1947 and has been in operation ever since. It's the only carousel in the District and the last one built with all jumping horses. (Ironically, the most popular seat on this merry-go-round is the sea dragon, which was added in 1996.)

A popular meeting place on the National Mall, the carousel is located in front of the Smithsonian Arts and Industries building. Rides are approximately three minutes long and cost around three dollars.

The carousel is open daily. The horses still go nowhere, but the kids have a lot of fun.

National Carousel
900 Jefferson Dr., SW, Washington, DC 20560
202-633-1000
www.nationalcarousel.com
Metro: Smithsonian (Blue, Silver, Orange lines)

WALK, RUN, OR SAIL
BY THE CHERRY BLOSSOMS IN BLOOM

The cherry trees are a treasure in DC. A gift from Japan, they grow in three locations: along the Tidal Basin, at Hains Point, and by the Washington Monument. And there are many ways to see these trees go from bud to bloom.

Attend the National Cherry Blossom Festival. Cherry blossoms are a fickle flower. It's hard to pin down the date when they'll be in bloom. The festival runs for several weeks to increase the chance of seeing the blossoms in full pink.

Run the Cherry Blossom Ten-Miler. This race is so popular that entry is by lottery only (which opens in December). Don't fret if you don't snag a slot; after two tries, you get an automatic berth. You can also increase your chances by entering with a group.

Cruise the Potomac. Board one of the many boats that offer charter cruises and see the cherry trees from the water.

National Cherry Blossom Festival
Tidal Basin Welcome Center
1501 Maine Ave., SW, Washington, DC 20024
1-877-44-BLOOM (25666)
www.nationalcherryblossomfestival.org
Metro: Smithsonian (Blue, Silver, Orange lines)

> **Visit the Tidal Basin early in
> the morning to avoid the crowds.**

RIDE YOUR SLED
DOWN BATTERY KEMBLE

DC doesn't get a lot of snow, but when it does, the hilly terrain around Battery Kemble Park is ideal for sledding. So throw your sled in the car and enjoy the fresh powder.

On sunnier days, you can check out the parapet and one-hundred-pound Parrott rifles preserved at the park from when it supported the city forts during the Civil War.

Battery Kemble Park
49th & Garfield Sts., NW, Washington, DC 20016
202-895-6070
www.nps.gov/cwdw/historyculture/battery-kemble.htm
Metro: Tenleytown (Red Line) is the closest, but still a good walk away.
There is parking nearby.

THREE MORE HILLS TO SLED ON

Capitol Hill
First St., SE, Washington, DC 20003
Metro: Capitol South (Blue, Silver, Orange lines)

Fort Reno Park (see page 32)
3800 Donaldson Pl., NW
Washington, DC 20018
Metro: Tenleytown (Red Line)

Rock Creek Park (see page 63)
23rd & P Sts., NW
Washington, DC 20037
Metro: Dupont Circle (Red Line)

SOLVE
THE POST HUNT

On the Sunday after Memorial Day, grab a copy of the *Washington Post Magazine* and go to Freedom Plaza for the annual Post Hunt, a live-action puzzle. The event kicks off at noon when Post Hunt creators deliver the first of six clues.

The first clue consists of five numbers. Combine the numbers with the five-letter answers from the set of opening questions inside the magazine. Then, set about with your team to solve five large-scale puzzles. You have three hours.

At 3 p.m., Post Hunt creators deliver EndGame, the final clue. The hunt cannot be solved without it. Shortly afterward, the winners are announced. First prize is $2,000.

How good are your puzzle-solving skills?

Post Hunt
Freedom Plaza
1455 Pennsylvania Ave., NW, Washington, DC 20004
www.washingtonpost.com/posthunt
Metro: Metro Center (Red Line)

SPLASH IN THE CANAL
AT YARDS PARK

On a hot, humid summer day, escape the heat at Yards Park, an outdoor entertainment center near Nationals Park. When you enter the park, you're greeted by a dancing fountain and a waterfall that cascades into an eleven-inch wading pool that mimics the historic canals in the District. Here you can splash and play in the summer sun.

Yards Park also features an open-air, tunnel-like bridge, an overlook above the Anacostia River, a boardwalk, a garden with wooden chaise lounges, and a performance terrace, plus restaurants and shops inside the park's three buildings: the Lumber Shed, the Foundry Lofts, and the Boilermaker Shops. There's even a trapeze school nearby.

Evenings are a great time to visit Yards Park. The fountains are illuminated, the boardwalk bustles and, on Fridays, concerts and special events are held on the terrace.

Yards Park
355 Water St., SE, Washington, DC 20003
202-465-7080
www.yardspark.org
Metro: Navy Yard (Green Line)

CELEBRATE THE SEASONS
AT LADY BIRD JOHNSON PARK

When you need a visual reminder of the beauty in the world, visit Lady Bird Johnson Park. In the spring, the island is an explosion of yellow daffodils and an array of tulips. In the fall, the trees sing in orange, red, and yellow. In the winter, it's blanketed in snow; in summer, it's covered in green.

The park is a beautiful place to have a picnic, to take photographs, to pass through on the Mount Vernon Trail, or just to enjoy a quiet retreat from the city.

There are two memorials located at Lady Bird Johnson Park—The Navy Marine Memorial and one for Lady Bird's husband, Lyndon Baines Johnson—along with a grove of white pines, landscaped paths, an open meadow, and an amazing view of the Washington Monument.

Lady Bird Johnson Park
www.nps.gov/gwmp/planyourvisit/ladybirdjohnsonpark.htm
Lyndon Baines Johnson Memorial Grove
www.nps.gov/lyba
Metro: Arlington Cemetery (Blue Line);
walk to the Columbia Island Marina

**Hungry? Grab a snack from the nearby
Columbia Island Marina.**

WATCH (OR RUN)
THE ROCK 'N' ROLL DC MARATHON

"If you are losing faith in human nature, go out and watch a marathon."—Kathrine Switzer

You'll have to rise and shine early for this race; runners come out before the sun does. The race starts near the National Mall and offers a rare chance to see the Washington Monument and Capitol Dome at sunrise.

The course weaves 13.1 miles for the half-marathon and 26.2 miles for the full marathon through the District, ending at RFK Stadium. There are bands throughout the course, many local, and a headliner at the end for a celebratory concert that runners and spectators alike will enjoy.

Rock 'n' Roll DC Marathon
www.runrocknroll.competitor.com/usa
Start: Constitution Ave., NW, just east of 14th St., NW
Metro: Federal Triangle, Smithsonian (Blue, Silver, Orange lines), Archives
(Yellow, Green lines), Metro Center (Red Line)
Finish: RFK Stadium Lot 7
Metro: Stadium/Armory station (Blue, Silver, Orange lines)

There's an enormous hill at mile five that's a great place to cheer runners on with a funny sign. They'll need it.

WHERE TO RUN IN DC

Washington, DC, is a great city for runners.
There are plenty of trails with
varied terrain. Here are the places
where you can run (or walk) in the District.

C&O Canal Towpath
Hains Point (see page 53)
National Mall
Potomac Heritage Trail
Roosevelt Island (see page 61)
Western Ridge and Valley Trails
Rock Creek Park

WATCH THE PRESIDENT'S RACE
AT THE WASHINGTON NATIONALS GAME

In the middle of the fourth inning during a Washington Nationals Major League Baseball game, the presidents take to the field—mascot presidents, that is. Wearing top-heavy costumes that just beg for a face plant in the dirt, the presidential mascots race their way around the outfield track toward the Nationals' bullpen.

Don't be alarmed if the presidents stop mid-race. They often pause to rally the crowd. Just pick your favorite—George, Tom, Abe, Teddy, or Bill (Taft)—and cheer him on to the finish line. Then go grab a beer and a half-smoke from the Ben's Chili Bowl kiosk and enjoy the rest of the game.

Nationals Park
1500 South Capitol St., NE, Washington, DC 20003
202-675-NATS (6287)
www.washington.nationals.mlb.com/was/fan_forum/presidents.jsp
Metro: Navy Yard-Ballpark (Green Line)

Want to go behind the scenes at Nationals Park? Take a tour, offered March-November on game days and not.

GET YOUR GAME ON
WITH DC'S OTHER PRO TEAMS

DC United
Major League Soccer
www.dcunited.com

Washington Redskins
National Football League
www.redskins.com

Washington Capitals
National Hockey League
capitals.nhl.com

Washington Wizards
National Basketball Association
www.nba.com/wizards

Washington Mystics
Women's National Basketball Association
www.wnba.com/mystics

SPEND SUNDAYS
WITH THE DRUM CIRCLE

Gather with friends and family on summer Sunday evenings in Meridian Hill Park and listen to the beat of the drum circle, a fifty-year DC tradition. Drummers and dancers have been performing in the park since Malcolm X was assassinated in 1965.

If you can keep the beat, you can even join in.

The park, which is sometimes referred to as Malcolm X Park, features the largest cascading fountain in North America, the only memorial to President James Buchanan in DC, and a Joan of Arc statue. Other notable statues include the Serenity statue near the park entrance and the statue of Dante Alighieri, author of *The Divine Comedy*, in the poetry corner.

While exploring the park, look for wayside displays, interactive exhibits throughout the park that tell its story.

Meridian Hill Park
16th St. & Euclid St., NW, Washington, DC 20009
202-895-6070
www.nps.gov/mehi/index.htm
Metro: Columbia Heights (Green, Yellow lines)

Learn more about Meridian Hill Park by taking the cell-phone tour. Dial 202-730-9307 and press one for a two-minute narration.

CULTURE AND HISTORY

HOP ON—AND OFF
THE OLD TOWN TROLLEY

Tour DC by trolley. The trolley tours allow you to hop on and off all day long, granting you time to explore while also transporting you easily from attraction to attraction.

Your feet will thank you.

Tours are narrated, which means you'll learn a lot more about your destination than if you'd taken the Metro. Attractions along the route include: Union Station, Library of Congress, Smithsonian, Jefferson and Lincoln Memorials, Washington Monument, White House, National Zoo, Ford's Theatre, and more.

Old Town Trolley also offers sunset and moonlight tours of the city, as well as the DC Duck tour, which explores the city by land and river.

Old Town Trolley
1-888-910-8687
www.trolleytours.com/washington-dc

DC Ducks
1-855-323-8257
www.dcducks.com

**Visit www.dcgps.trolleytours.com
to track the trolley and find out when the next
one will arrive at your location.**

MORE HOP-ON-AND-OFF OPTIONS

Big Bus
www.eng.bigbustours.com/international/home.html

CitySights DC
www.citysightsdc.com

DC Circulator
www.dccirculator.com

Grayline
www.graylinedc.com

ATTEND
THE PRESIDENTIAL INAUGURATION

It only happens once every four years. Make sure you experience the pomp and circumstance of this uniquely American ceremony at least once. Request tickets from your Congressional representative or US senators, or stake out your spot in the crowd on the National Mall.

US Capitol, West Front Terrace
East Capitol and First Sts., SE, Washington, DC 20004
202-226-8000
www.inaugural.senate.gov

Skip the swearing-in ceremony for the Inaugural Parade, also free, and catch a glimpse of the president from the sidewalks along Pennsylvania and Constitution avenues.

BE A KID AGAIN
AT THE NATIONAL BUILDING MUSEUM

Play is at the forefront of the National Building Museum experience. Walk into the great hall and you'll likely see children building an archway or families tinkering with a tool kit.

Did you play with blocks when you were a child? From small blocks to big-as-a-kid blocks to virtual blocks, the Play Work Build exhibit is a hands-on playground for would-be architects and engineers. There's even a collection of architectural toys, featuring the very presidential Lincoln Logs. The exhibit is meant for children and adults.

For kids two to six, the Building Zone provides an age-appropriate introduction. For grown-ups, the interactive experience spills over into the House & Home exhibit, which explores what defines a home.

The answer may surprise you.

National Building Museum
401 F St., NW, Washington, DC 20001
202-272-2448
www.nbm.org
Metro: Judiciary Square (Red Line), Gallery Place-Chinatown
(Red, Yellow, Green lines)

**Admission to the House & Home
exhibit is free after 4 p.m.**

FIND
THE HIDDEN MEMORIALS

Sure, you could visit the famous memorials in DC, or you could seek out the lesser-known ones hidden in plain sight around town. Here are a few that should be on your must-see list.

African American Civil War Memorial & Museum
1925 Vermont Ave., NW
Washington, DC 20001
Metro: U Street, Shaw-Howard U
(Yellow, Green lines)

Albert Einstein Memorial
2101 Constitution Ave., NW
Washington, DC 20418
Metro: Foggy Bottom (Blue, Silver, Orange lines)

The Extra Mile—Points of Light Volunteer Pathway
15th St. & Pennsylvania Ave. to
15th & G Sts., NW
Washington, DC 20005
Metro: Metro Center (Red Line)
McPherson Square (Blue, Silver, Orange lines)

Victims of Communism Memorial
Massachusetts & New Jersey Aves., NW
Washington, DC 20001
Metro: Union Station (Red Line)

Jefferson Pier at the Washington Monument
Constitution Ave. & 16th St., NW
Washington, DC 20007
Metro: Federal Triangle (Blue, Silver, Orange lines)

"Motherland," the Armenian Earthquake Statue
North Lawn of the American Red Cross Headquarters
430 17th St., NW
Washington, DC 20008
Metro: Farragut West (Blue, Silver, Orange lines)

Zero Milestone Marker
North Edge of the President's Park Ellipse
Washington, DC 20001
Metro: Federal Triangle, McPherson Square (Blue, Silver, Orange lines), Metro Center (Red, Blue, Silver, Orange lines)

Find them all here: www.ncpc.gov/memorials

CHANNEL YOUR INNER
BOND, JAMES BOND

Step into the disguise of your favorite spy and explore the International Spy Museum as a secret agent. Inside this interactive museum, you'll be immersed in espionage.

Your journey as a spy begins at the Covers & Legends checkpoint, where you'll assume your new identity. Then, after a trip to the Briefing Room, you'll go on to spy school and learn the history of espionage and tricks of the trade.

At the end of your adventure, you'll view over one hundred artifacts from fifty years of 007 movies and discover how Bond, James Bond, and the villains he battled compare to real-life spies.

If you want the full spy experience, don't miss Operation Spy, a live-action spy adventure, and Spy in the City, a GPS tour of DC through the eyes of a cyber-spy.

Trench coats and sunglasses sold separately.

International Spy Museum
800 F St., NW, Washington, DC 20004
202-654-0950
www.spymuseum.org
Metro: Gallery Place-Chinatown (Red, Yellow, Green lines)

Plan your visit for a weekday and take the kids on a secret mission. Download the Family Mission Guide before you go, or pick up a copy at the museum.

CREATE A RUBBING
OF A MEMORIAL WALL

Visit the National Law Enforcement Officers Memorial and you'll find paper and pencil alongside the directory of names. Use them to create a rubbing of the wall. Place the paper over the names engraved on the memorial and lightly shade the paper with the side of your number two. The resulting pencil "photograph" is a simple way to create a tangible reminder of sacrifices made and to remember loved ones lost.

The National Law Enforcement Officers Memorial, with its wall of names and four powerful lion statues, is a must-see anytime of year, but especially in May during National Police Week. This is when new names are added to the wall.

At the Vietnam Veterans Memorial, over 58,000 names are etched in the wall. A directory of names is also available here, but you'll need to supply your own pencil and paper to make a keepsake. Be respectful.

National Law Enforcement Officers Memorial
E St. between 4th & 5th Sts., NW, Washington, DC 20011
www.nleomf.org/memorial
Metro: Judiciary Square (Red Line)

Vietnam Veterans Memorial
Henry Bacon Dr., NW, Washington, DC 20007
www.nps.gov/vive/index.htm
Metro: L'Enfant Plaza (Yellow, Green lines)

● ●

DEFEND THE DISTRICT
ON A CIVIL WAR TRAIL

By the end of the Civil War, DC was home to eighty-six forts, collectively known as the Civil War Defenses. Fort Stevens was the only one of those to see active fighting. Confederate soldiers attacked the fort in July 1864, only to withdraw two days later. Today, the fort is partially reconstructed and part of a network of twenty preserved forts.

You can see five of the forts, including Fort Stevens, by hiking the Civil War Defenses Trail from Fort Reno to Fort Totten. The nearly six-mile hike travels sidewalks and wooded paths, passing through Rock Creek Park and Tenley Circle. There are Metro stations at each endpoint, so you don't need to walk back.

Civil War Defenses Trail
Start: Fort Reno
Metro: Tenleytown (Red Line)
End: Fort Totten
Metro: Fort Totten (Red, Yellow, Green lines)
www.nps.gov/pohe/planyourvisit/civil_war_defenses.htm

The hike is self-guided. Download the guide from the NPS website before you go. It contains route and historical information.

DISCOVER
DC'S STONEHENGE

Nestled between Michigan Avenue and North Capitol, Channing, and First Streets is McMillan Park, a twenty-five-acre property that was home to the city's water filtration plant until the mid-1980s. The Sand Filtration Plant was one of the last in the United States. Today, the park is under development, but the sand filtration silos still tower in rows. Beneath the ivy-covered silos are vault-like chambers where sand filtered water from the Potomac.

The park, which is listed on the National Register of Historic Places, is not open to the public, but the Stonehenge-like silos can easily be seen from its perimeter. The original park was designed by Frederick Law Olmsted Jr. and featured green space for recreation, a walkway around the reservoir, and a fountain.

McMillan Park Reservoir Historic District
N. Capitol St., NW, Michigan Ave., NW, First St., NW, and
Channing St., NW, Washington, DC 20010
www.nps.gov/nr/feature/places/13000022.htm
Metro: Brookland-CUA (Red Line)

EXPERIENCE
THE REAL-LIFE CSI

If you love the CBS drama *CSI: Crime Scene Investigation*, then you must visit the Crime Museum in DC. Even if you're not a fan of the show, all crime buffs must put this museum at the top of their list of places to visit in the District.

The interactive museum features a CSI lab, an FBI training center, a high-speed police chase simulator, artifacts, exhibits about notorious criminals, and the *America's Most Wanted* stage set, all on three floors near the Verizon Center.

While the subject matter is dark, the museum itself is actually kid-friendly for ages six and up. There are Q&A stops positioned at eye level throughout the museum that address questions about safety, and there's an interactive scavenger hunt that lets kids be the detective.

Crime Museum
575 7th St., NW, Washington, DC 20004
202-393-1099
www.crimemuseum.org
Metro: Gallery Place-Chinatown (Red, Yellow, Green lines)

CSI SLEEPOVER
The Crime Museum also offers overnights for groups.

EXPERIENCE ART
ON THE FRINGE

Where can you experience avant-garde art at an affordable price? At the annual Capital Fringe Festival held throughout the month of July.

A fringe festival is a cutting-edge celebration of the performing arts. Performances are innovative, pushing the creative envelope for both artist and audience, and vary in genre from theater to dance to the spoken word.

Think uncensored, modern interpretations of the classics and out-of-the box skits about contemporary topics.

The mission of Capital Fringe is to connect artists with audiences. They do this through their Fringe Factory and the festival, one of the largest fringe festivals in the United States. Ticket prices are kept low on purpose so that performances are accessible to all.

Open your mind to the fringe and enjoy the show.

Capital Fringe
1358 Florida Ave., NE, Washington, DC 20002
866-811-4111
www.capitalfringe.org
Metro: NoMa-Gallaudet (Red Line)

> **Your Capital Fringe Button, which gets you into the festival, also grants you discounts at venues around the city throughout the year.**

SPEND THE NIGHT
AT THE MUSEUM

Unroll your sleeping bag for an overnight at the Smithsonian. Sleepovers are held at both the American History Museum and the Natural History Museum during the summer months for children ages eight-twelve with an adult (there's your in, moms and dads).

At the American History Museum, kids play detective while exploring the museum for clues to solve a crime. Then they play president before going to bed. At the Natural History Museum, kids explore the museum, participate in crafts, and watch an IMAX film before going to sleep. Both sleepovers include breakfast, but not dinner.

So, the question remains: Would you rather sleep beside the Star-Spangled Banner or beneath Phoenix the whale? Both are sure to be experiences you won't soon forget.

Smithsonian Sleepovers
202-633-3030
www.smithsoniansleepovers.org
Metro: Federal Triangle (Blue, Silver, Orange lines)

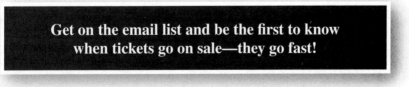

Get on the email list and be the first to know when tickets go on sale—they go fast!

FIND DARTH VADER
AT THE NATIONAL CATHEDRAL

Grab your binoculars and aim them toward the northwest tower of the Washington National Cathedral. Up high sits a grotesque of Darth Vader. A grotesque is like a gargoyle; it serves to deflect rain. While gargoyles deflect rain through a pipe in their mouth, grotesques deflect rain when it bounces off their head.

The Darth Vader grotesque came to be during construction of the tower in the 1980s. The cathedral, along with *National Geographic*, hosted a decorative design competition for kids. The *Star Wars* villain was sculpted from one of the winning designs. The other winning designs—a raccoon, a girl, and a man with an umbrella—can be spotted nearby.

Self-guided tours of the gargoyles are available year round. Guided tours are offered April through October.

Washington National Cathedral
3101 Wisconsin Ave., NW, Washington, DC 20016
202-537-6200
www.nationalcathedral.org
Metro: Tenleytown/AU (Red Line); transfer to a thirty series bus or walk
1.5 miles down Wisconsin Avenue

**Look for Vader high above the statue of
Abraham Lincoln.**

HOUSES OF WORSHIP WORTH THE TRIP

National Shrine of the Immaculate Conception
400 Michigan Ave., NE, Washington, DC 20017
202-536-8300
www.nationalshrine.com
Metro: Brookland/CUA (Red Line)

Franciscan Monastery
1400 Quincy St., NE, Washington, DC 20017
202-526-6800
www.myfranciscan.org
Metro: Brookland/CUA (Red Line)

FIND
FAMOUS FACES

Stand in one of the seventeen galleries that comprise the "American Origins" exhibit at the National Portrait Gallery and you'll see the story of our country staring back at you.

As its name suggests, the portrait gallery focuses on faces, some famous and some not, and celebrates the people who shape our country, sharing their stories through portraiture.

The museum itself is a national historic landmark, having once housed the US Patent Office, and it is home to the only complete collection of presidential portraits outside of the White House. However, the exhibits aren't limited to portraits of historical figures. Many contemporary figures are celebrated, too. See their portraits at the "Contemporary Americans," "Champions," and "Bravo!" exhibits.

National Portrait Gallery
8th & F Sts., NW, Washington, DC 20001
202-633-8300
www.npg.si.edu
Metro: Gallery Place-Chinatown (Red, Yellow, Green lines)

Don't miss the Kogod courtyard. It's gorgeous!

HAVE LUNCH
WITH THE FIRST LADY

The First Lady Luncheon is an annual event hosted by the Congressional Club. Tickets are invitation only and are hard to come by, unless you are a club member, which means you are married to a member of Congress.

The Congressional Club is the official club of congressional spouses. It was incorporated by Congress in 1908. In 1912, the club hosted a breakfast to honor First Lady Helen Taft, beginning a tradition that has since evolved from breakfast to lunch. Today, the club has nearly 700 members, each of whom gets four tickets to the luncheon.

This prestigious event, which happens every spring, is formal, with guests decked out in the finest fashions, and features a gourmet meal, goodie bag, star-powered entertainment, and, of course, the first lady of the United States.

Congressional Club
First Lady Luncheon
www.thecongressionalclub.com

FOLLOW IN THE FOOTSTEPS
OF DR. MARTIN LUTHER KING JR.

On August 28, 1963, Dr. Martin Luther King Jr. delivered his "I Have a Dream" speech on the steps of the Lincoln Memorial to a crowd of 250,000. Stand where he stood when you visit the memorial—there's a plaque that marks the spot—look out on the Reflecting Pool, and imagine the magic of that day. Then visit Dr. King's memorial, which was dedicated forty-eight years to the day after his famous speech.

At the memorial, you'll see a larger-than-life sculpture of Dr. King carved from a granite block and quotes that tell his story and pay tribute to the civil rights leader. The memorial is moving any time of year. In the spring, it offers a stunning view of the cherry trees around the Tidal Basin.

Lincoln Memorial
2 Lincoln Memorial Cir., NW
Washington, DC 20037
202-426-6841
www.nps.gov/linc
Metro: Foggy Bottom
(Blue, Silver, Orange lines)

Martin Luther King Jr. Memorial
1964 Independence Ave., SW
Washington, DC 20024
202-426-6841
www.nps.gov/mlkm
Metro: Smithsonian
(Blue, Silver, Orange lines)

Honor Dr. King by volunteering during the Martin Luther King Jr. Day of Service in January.

GET INSPIRED
BY FDR

"There is nothing so American as our national parks."—Franklin Delano Roosevelt (1936)

Given his sentiments, it's fitting that the thirty-second president of the United States is enshrined at a national park; his memorial is located on the western shore of the Tidal Basin.

As you walk through the memorial, you'll travel through the four terms of FDR's presidency, reading his story—as told in his own words—etched along a granite wall. The memorial features ten bronze statues, waterfalls, and quiet pools and is entirely wheelchair accessible.

It's a beautiful place to visit and contemplate the important things in life. Go see it in the evening as the light is fading and enjoy the peacefulness.

Franklin Delano Roosevelt Memorial
400 W. Basin Dr., SW, Washington, DC 20242
www.nps.gov/frde
Metro: Smithsonian (Blue, Silver, Orange lines)

GET YOUR HANDS
ON AMERICAN HISTORY

Families love the Smithsonian's American History Museum because there are so many hands-on activities for kids and grownups alike. (Look for the hands-on carts throughout the museum.) Docents demonstrate historical activities like how to use a printing press and a cotton gin and give you a chance to try them out, too.

Another great draw for the whole family is the "Star-Spangled Banner" exhibit. In addition to the Old Glory, there's an interactive table that explains how the flag was made.

For more interactive fun, visit the "America on the Move" exhibit, where you can "ride" a Chicago L train and travel along Route 66; "The American Presidency" exhibit, where you can step up to the podium and deliver a presidential address; and the "Within These Walls" exhibit, where you can step inside a reconstructed Georgian-style house.

The National Museum of American History
14th St. & Constitution Ave., NW, Washington, DC 20001
202-633-1000
www.americanhistory.si.edu
Metro: Federal Triangle, Smithsonian (Blue, Silver, Orange lines)

MORE MUST-SEE EXHIBITS AT THE AMERICAN HISTORY MUSEUM

Gunboat Philadelphia

The First Ladies and the Gallery of Gowns

"American Stories," featuring
Dorothy's Ruby Slippers

"Food: Transforming the American Table," which
showcases Julia Child's Kitchen

*Pick up the family guide to the "America
on the Move" exhibit at
the Welcome Center.*

GO ON AN ARMCHAIR ADVENTURE
WITH NATIONAL GEOGRAPHIC

Best known for stunning photography from around the world, *National Geographic* is much more than a magazine. It's a source of adventure for armchair travelers.

Nat Geo Live, a series of live events, brings that adventure to you through entertaining concerts, films, and talks held at an intimate theater inside National Geographic headquarters. Past events include a farm-to-table talk with a photographer and a best-of showing of films from Mountainfilm in Telluride.

The National Geographic Museum is also worth a visit. The interactive exhibits bring the pages of the magazine to life and let you live vicariously through the adventures of others.

National Geographic Live
Gilbert H. Grosvenor Auditorium
1600 M St., NW, Washington, DC 20036
202-857-7700
www.events.nationalgeographic.com/events/locations/
center/grosvenor-auditorium
Metro: Farragut North (Red Line)

National Geographic Museum
1145 17th St., NW, Washington, DC 20036
202-857-7588
www.events.nationalgeographic.com/events/national-geographic-museum
Metro: Farragut North (Red Line)

MAKE IT A DATE NIGHT!

Get dinner before the show at one of these nearby restaurants and enjoy a discount by presenting your ticket. See page 30 for more date-night ideas.

Beacon Bar & Grill
1615 Rhode Island Ave., NW, Washington, DC 20036
202-872-1126
www.bbgwdc.com
Metro: Farragut North (Red Line)

Daily Grill
1200 18th St., NW, Washington, DC 20036
202-822-5282
www.dailygrill.com/locations/
daily-grill-washington-district-of-columbia
Metro: Farragut North (Red Line)

Dupont Italian Kitchen
1637 17th St., NW, Washington, DC 20009
202-328-3222
www.dupontitaliankitchen.com
Metro: Dupont Circle (Red Line)

Nage
1600 Rhode Island Ave., NW, Washington, DC 20036
202-448-8005
www.nagedc.com
Metro: Farragut North (Red Line)

HANG OUT
WITH THE BUTTERFLIES

Have you ever had a butterfly land on your finger? Don't be surprised if this happens inside the Butterfly Pavilion at the Smithsonian's National Museum of Natural History. Here, you'll get up close and personal with hundreds of live butterflies.

Inside the cocoon-like pavilion, 400 butterflies sip nectar from flowers and fly from plant to plant—and sometimes to people. The butterflies come from farms in Africa, Asia, and North and South America and represent thirty species. New butterflies are introduced weekly.

The pavilion is located next to the insect zoo and is a paid part of "Partners in Evolution," a free exhibition about insects, animals, and plants. Admission to the butterfly pavilion ranges from $5-6, except on Tuesdays, when it's free. A timed-entry ticket is required no matter when you go.

Butterfly Pavilion
National Museum of Natural History
10th St. & Constitution Ave., NW, Washington, DC 20004
202-633-1000
www.butterflies.si.edu
Metro: Smithsonian (Blue, Silver, Orange lines)

TIPS

- Purchases your tickets before you go.
- Get there early so you don't miss your entry time.
- Park your stroller or leave it at home. Strollers are not allowed inside.
- Store your coat. The climate-controlled pavilion is warm and humid.

• •

BUTTERFLY HABITAT GARDEN

On the east side the Natural History Museum, you'll find an outdoor oasis filled with butterflies. Stroll through the garden on your own or take a tour, offered weekly April through September.

9th St. between Constitution Ave. & the National Mall
Washington, DC 20004
www.gardens.si.edu/our-gardens/butterfly-habitat-garden.html

MARVEL
AT MODERN ART

Inside the concrete sphere that is the Hirshhorn are more than 12,000 pieces of art that will make you tilt your head and ponder the works' meaning.

Part of the Smithsonian family, the Hirshhorn is a contemporary and modern art museum featuring artists from the late-ninteenth century to the present. The museum is also home to "one of the most comprehensive collections of modern sculptures in the world," which can be viewed inside the museum and in its sculpture garden.

The Hirshhorn is known for its variety of programs, including the Meet the Artist Series, Friday Gallery Talks, ARTWORKS, and the Independent Film Program (the first in the country) hosted in the Gustave and Marion Ring Auditorium.

Hirshhorn Museum and Sculpture Garden
7th St. & Independence Ave., SW, Washington, DC 20560
202-633-4674
www.hirshhorn.si.edu
Metro: L'Enfant Plaza (Blue, Silver, Orange, Yellow, Green lines)

Plan your visit for a Saturday or Sunday to participate in one of the afternoon tours.

MEET ABLE,
THE SPACE MONKEY

The National Air and Space Museum is home to Able, a preserved rhesus monkey who rode into space on May 28, 1959. She and her flight companion, Baker, a squirrel monkey, were the first astronaut monkeys to survive space travel. Unfortunately, Able died shortly afterward during a routine surgical procedure. She was preserved and is on display in the "Apollo to the Moon" exhibit at the museum, along with the biocapsules that transported her and Baker into space. Baker lived long after their 1959 flight. She died in 1984 and is buried at the US Space Center & Rocket Center, a Smithsonian affiliate, in Huntsville, Alabama.

In addition, the exhibit features spacecraft and equipment used on various missions during the program, including the spacesuits worn by the astronauts on the moon.

Smithsonian National Air and Space Museum
600 Independence Ave., SW, Washington, DC 20560
202-633-2214
www.airandspace.si.edu
Metro: L'Enfant Plaza (Yellow, Green lines)

PAY YOUR RESPECTS

Arlington National Cemetery in Virginia tops many lists of must-see places in Washington, DC. However, there are several cemeteries inside the District that also warrant a visit.

Arlington National Cemetery
Arlington, VA 22211, 877-907-8585
Metro: Arlington Cemetery (Blue Line)

What's notable: Changing of the Guard, John F. Kennedy gravesite, and the Tomb of the Unknowns.

Congressional Cemetery
1801 E St., SE, Washington, DC 20003, 202-543-0539
Metro: Potomac Avenue (Blue, Silver, Orange lines)

What's notable: Final resting place for many politicians, including Presidents William H. Harrison and John Quincy Adams. Free tours Saturday at 11 a.m., April-October.

Oak Hill Cemetery
30th & R Sts., NW, Washington, DC 20007
Metro: Foggy Bottom (Blue, Silver, Orange lines)

What's notable: the chapel, the Van Ness Mausoleum, and the E.M. Stanton monument.

Rock Creek Cemetery
Rock Creek Church Rd. & Webster St., NW
Washington, DC 20011, 202-726-2080
Metro: Georgia Avenue-Petworth (Yellow, Green lines)

What's notable: Final resting place of many noteworthy Washington residents, including Charles Corby, the creator of Wonder Bread, and author Upton Sinclair.

Soldiers' Home
21 Harewood Rd., NW, Washington, DC 20011, 1-877-907-8585
Metro: Georgia Avenue-Petworth (Yellow, Green lines)

What's notable: one of the oldest national cemeteries and the final resting place of more than 14,000 veterans, including twenty-one recipients of the Medal of Honor.

RETRACE
LINCOLN'S LAST STEPS

Experience the legacy of President Abraham Lincoln at Ford's Theatre. The tour is so much more than a backstage pass to the theatre where Lincoln was assassinated. It's a celebration of his presidency.

Start your tour in the museum. Follow Lincoln from his arrival in Washington in 1861, through the Civil War, to the night he was shot. Continue to the theatre and see Lincoln's box. Then, head across the street to the Peterson House to see where the president died.

End your tour at the Center for Education and Leadership. Be sure to take the stairs as you go from gallery to gallery. The winding staircase wraps around the Lincoln Book Tower, a thirty-four-foot tower of books about the man. You won't see anything like it anywhere but DC.

Ford's Theatre
511 Tenth St., NW, Washington, DC 20004
202-347-4833, www.fordstheatre.org
Metro: Metro Center (Red, Blue, Silver, Orange lines),
Gallery Place-Chinatown (Red, Yellow, Green lines),
Archives-Navy Memorial (Yellow, Green lines)

Admission is free, but tickets are required.
Grab the family guide if you're visiting with kids.
Deepen your experience by taking a History on Foot walking tour or watching a performance at the theatre.

PLAY REPORTER
AT THE NEWSEUM

Get ready to deliver the news in three, two, one . . .

At the Newseum, you can report live from the White House, the Newseum, or the Cherry Blossom Festival, or share the weather forecast from the NBC News Interactive Newsroom. Just follow the teleprompter (it's fast!) and smile for the camera. Your thirty-second clip will then play back on the television screens. You can even upload your broadcast to YouTube and share it with your friends.

The Newseum is so much more than a newsroom. It's packed full of exhibits that explore history through the lens of the media. The exhibits touch on significant world events like the fall of the Berlin Wall, the Civil Rights Movement, and 9/11.

Don't miss the Pulitzer Prize-winning-photographs gallery, the great book display, and clips of comedians broadcasting the news.

Newseum
555 Pennsylvania Ave., NW, Washington, DC 20001
202-292-6100
www.newseum.org
Metro: Archives-Navy Memorial-Penn Quarter
(Yellow, Green lines), Judiciary Square (Red Line)

Tickets are good for two consecutive days. Time your visit for when a new exhibit opens to maximize the experience.

SEE THE FINER THINGS
AT HILLWOOD

If you've ever wondered how the other half lives, spend an afternoon exploring the rooms of Hillwood Estate, the Georgian-style mansion that was once home to Post Cereal heiress Marjorie Merriweather Post. The house is a museum furnished as it was when Post lived there.

Her estate is home to the precious items she collected throughout her life, including eighteenth-century French decorative art, Cartier jewelry, and the "most comprehensive collection of Russian imperial art outside of Russia." These pieces can be seen throughout the house, from the French drawing room to the Russian porcelain room to her bedroom suite.

Outside her home are thirteen acres of gardens organized in a series of outdoor rooms that flow from the secluded French Parterre to the rose garden to the circular Four Seasons Overlook, all by way of the English Garden Friendship Walk.

Hillwood Estate Museum & Gardens
4155 Linnean Ave., NW, Washington, DC 20008
202-686-5807
www.hillwoodmuseum.org
Metro: Van Ness-UDC (Red Line); it's a one-mile walk to Hillwood

> **Plan your visit for March and get an early glimpse of spring inside the greenhouse when it's abloom with orchids.**

REMEMBER
THE CHILDREN WHO SURVIVED
THE HOLOCAUST

Warning: a visit to the US Holocaust Memorial Museum is wrought with emotion. That said, the experience will move you, and that's what makes it so worthwhile.

If you're a sensitive soul, "Remember the Children: Daniel's Story" is an exhibit that approaches the subject matter delicately. The exhibit tells the story of the Holocaust through the eyes of a young boy.

As you walk through the exhibit, you'll travel through Daniel's world as it changes during the Nazi regime. You can read Daniel's diary, peek inside his family's hiding place, and walk through a concentration camp.

Daniel's Story is appropriate for children age eight or older; however, children should be at least eleven years old to view the permanent exhibits in other areas of the museum.

United States Holocaust Memorial Museum
100 Raoul Wallenberg Place, SW, Washington, DC 20024
202-488-0400
www.ushmm.org
Metro: Smithsonian (Blue, Silver, Orange lines)

TIP

Preview Daniel's Story before you go.
www.ushmm.org/information/exhibitions/
museum-exhibitions/remember-the-
children-daniels-story/video

Admission is free but timed-entry passes
are required during the museum's peak
season, March through August. The
best time of year to visit the museum is
September through February.
Note: The museum is closed on
Yom Kippur and
Christmas Day.

STROLL THROUGH
DUMBARTON OAKS

On a sunny day, take a stroll through the gardens at Dumbarton Oaks and be inspired by their beauty. The historic gardens were originally created by landscape designer Beatrix Farrand for the Bliss family, who purchased the property in 1920. Some of the gardens are enclosed, while others are less defined.

On your visit, pause inside the Ellipse to enjoy the peace and quiet of the garden. Then continue to the Forsythia Dell, golden in the spring, and rest on the friend benches.

Travel the Prunus Walk to the Orchard. Then pass through the Urn Terrace to the Rose Garden, where 900 roses grow. Or follow Melisande's Allée, a wide brick path, to Lover's Lane Pool, a natural pond and amphitheater.

Before you leave, find the Bliss family motto engraved in stone inside the Pebble Garden.

Dumbarton Oaks
1703 32nd St., NW, Washington, DC 20007
202-339-6401
www.doaks.org
Metro: Dupont Circle (Red Line), Foggy Bottom (Blue, Silver, Orange lines); walk or transfer to a Metrobus or Circulator bus.

STEP BACK
TO THE FEDERAL ERA

Not to be confused with Dumbarton Oaks, the Dumbarton House Museum is a Federal-style house that shows what life was like when Washington, DC, was a new capital city. Open as a historic house museum since 1932, it exemplifies the era in its architecture and décor. In 1814, the house, then known as Belle Vue, provided sanctuary to First Lady Dolley Madison as she fled the White House during the War of 1812. Today, the house is part of the Star-Spangled Banner Historic Trail, which commemorates the War of 1812. The property also features an adjacent park and herb garden planted with flora that flourished in the eighteenth and nineteenth centuries. Admission costs $5 for adults and is free for children.

Dumbarton House
2715 Q St., NW, Washington, DC 20007
202-337-2288
www.dumbartonhouse.org
Metro: Dupont Circle (Red Line)

SEE WHERE
LINCOLN SUMMERED

During Abraham Lincoln's presidency, he escaped the heat of wartime Washington by living in a cottage three miles from the White House. From early summer through the fall months, he commuted daily by horseback and worked on the Emancipation Proclamation and the 13th Amendment.

Today, Lincoln's cottage is part of the Soldiers' Home, the Armed Forces Retirement Home for veterans. The property features a life-size bronze of Lincoln and his horse. Guided tours of the house are available to the public by reservation.

The tour shows what life was like for the Lincolns during those summers, detailing their daily routines and examining the issues the president dealt with during the Civil War.

Tickets are required to tour the house. Be sure to arrive early and bring a photo ID.

President Lincoln's Cottage at the Soldiers' Home
140 Rock Creek Church Rd., NW, Washington, DC 20011
202-829-0436
www.lincolncottage.org
Metro: Georgia Avenue-Petworth (Yellow, Green lines)

Visit Lincoln's Cottage in early October to enjoy the annual Fall Fest.

SPEND FRIDAYS
AT THE ARTS CLUB OF WASHINGTON

Next Friday at noon, head over to the Arts Club of Washington for their Friday Noon Concert series. The half-hour concert, which is free and open to the public, features vocal and/or instrumental performances. The club has hosted more than 600 such concerts.

Set inside a Federal-style townhouse, the Arts Club of Washington is more than just a concert hall. It's an art gallery— four, in fact—and a historic mansion that was once home to President James Monroe.

If you have time, spend your Friday afternoon touring the galleries inside the historic house turned home of the arts. The galleries showcase national and regional artists, as well as member artists. The first Friday of the month typically brings the opening of a new exhibit.

Arts Club of Washington
2017 I St., NW, Washington, DC 20006
202-331-7282
www.artsclubofwashington.org/calendar/friday-noon-concerts
Metro: Farragut North (Red Line)

The Arts Club of Washington also hosts workshops, classes, and a monthly series: Evening with an Extraordinary Artist. See their calendar for more information.

CELEBRATE
SHAKESPEARE'S BIRTHDAY

The historic reading rooms at the Folger Shakespeare Library are open to the public just one day a year—during the library's annual celebration of Shakespeare's birthday in April. The free event, billed as an open house, is held rain or shine.

You'll see jugglers and jesters and even Queen Elizabeth I; her majesty presides over the birthday-cake-cutting ceremony. You'll also enjoy sword fighting, sonnets, and short Shakespeare performances.

The Folger is home to the world's largest collection of Shakespeare materials. It serves as a hub for researchers, but is also open to the public for tours of the building, exhibits, and Elizabethan garden. Exhibit highlights include a first-edition collection of Shakespeare's plays, many of which are regularly performed in the elegant, Elizabethan-style Folger Theatre.

Folger Shakespeare Library
201 East Capitol St., SE, Washington, DC 20003
202-544-7077
www.folger.edu
Metro: Union Station (Red Line)

Want more Shakespeare?
Attend a performance by the Shakespeare Theatre Company
at the Harman Center for the Arts. www.shakespearetheatre.org

SEE THE WORLD'S
LARGEST STAMP GALLERY

Stamp collectors, get ready to geek out. The largest stamp gallery in the world is located in DC. The 12,000-square-foot William H. Gross Stamp Gallery at the National Postal Museum houses reproductions of fifty-four historic US stamps displayed in the windows overlooking Massachusetts Avenue.

Some of the notable stamps on display in the gallery are the 1840 Penny Black, the inverted Jenny, one of only two 1868 one-cent Z-grill stamps in existence, Dr. Martin Luther King's "I Have a Dream" speech stamp, and the bestselling 1993 Elvis stamp.

The museum itself explores the history of postage from the sixteen hundreds to the present through interactive exhibits, including a stagecoach you can ride and a 1920s post office that you can explore. You can even start (or add to) your own stamp collection.

National Postal Museum
2 Massachusetts Ave., NE, Washington, DC 20002
202-633-5555
www.postalmuseum.si.edu
Metro: Union Station (Red Line)

STAND BENEATH
THE CAPITOL DOME

To enter the US Capitol, you must first go underground. The entrance to the Capitol Visitors Center is located under the east front plaza. This new facility was built underground so as not to distract from the building's iconic exterior.

The visitors center is where all tours of the US Capitol begin and end. It's also home to the exhibition hall, a restaurant, and gift shops.

On the forty-five-minute tour, you'll view a short film before seeing the Rotunda and the National Statuary Hall. The hall houses two statues from each state.

In addition to the general tour, there are specialty tours: a walking tour outdoors, a Civil War tour, and a tour of the Brumidi Corridors, ornate hallways on the first floor of the Senate wing.

US Capitol & Visitors Center
East Capitol St., NE & First St., SE, Washington, DC 20004
202-226-8000
www.visitthecapitol.gov
Metro: Union Station (Red Line)

**Tours must be booked in advance.
Book yours online at www.tours.visitthecapitol.gov.**

SEE HISTORY IN THE MAKING

If you'd like to visit the House and Senate galleries, you'll need to request a pass from your state's senators or representatives. The galleries are not included in the US Capitol tour.

SEE THE MEMORIALS
AT NIGHT

Washington, DC, is known for its iconic—and numerous—memorials. While beautiful in daylight, they're even more spectacular at night. Some of the ones best admired in the dark include the Jefferson, Lincoln, and Korean War memorials.

There are several ways to see these memorials illuminated. One is to take a self-guided driving tour around the city. Another is to take a night tour of the city offered by the various tour bus and sightseeing companies that operate from Union Station.

You can also take a walking tour. Washington Walks offers Memorials By Moonlight tours during summer weekends. There are three tours: around the Tidal Basin, along the Reflecting Pool, and on the National Mall.

Washington Walks
202-484-1565
www.washingtonwalks.com

VISIT
THE OLDEST HOUSE IN THE DISTRICT

On M Street in Georgetown is the oldest building in DC, and you can take a look inside. The aptly named Old Stone House is an originally maintained structure from the Revolutionary War era. The structure gives a glimpse back at the lives of Georgetown residents during the seventeen hundreds and eighteen hundreds.

Take a self-guided tour of the property, which includes an English garden and bookstore. (The bookstore occupies space that was once a clock shop.)

While you're in the neighborhood, take a walk through Herring Hill on the African American Heritage Trail (see page 60 for more about heritage trails). More than 1,000 families settled in the neighborhood after the Civil War and established many of the churches, homes, and schools that exist there today.

The Old Stone House
3051 M St., NW, Washington, DC 20007
www.nps.gov/olst
Metro: Foggy Bottom (Blue, Silver, Orange lines); transfer to Metrobus

TAKE A MULE-DRAWN
BOAT RIDE ON THE C&O

Once upon a time, there was a canal boat, aptly named the *Georgetown*, that took visitors to Georgetown on a historic ride along the C&O Canal. Sadly, the Georgetown sailed her last tour in 2012. But, don't despair. You can still ride a mule-drawn canal boat, so long as you don't mind crossing the District line into Maryland.

Just eight miles from Georgetown, you can board *The Charles F. Mercer* at the Great Falls Visitors Center for an hour-long boat ride on the C&O Canal. Mules pull the boats on the weekends from April to October while park rangers in period costumes talk about life on the canal in the 1870s.

Great Falls Canal Boat Ride
11710 MacArthur Blvd., Potomac, MD 20854
301-767-3714
www.nps.gov/choh/planyourvisit/great-falls-canal-boat-rides.htm
Metro: There's no Metro to Great Falls. Instead, take M Street to MacArthur Boulevard and travel eight miles to the park's visitor center.

Seats are first-come, first-serve. Call or check the website before you go, as the schedule is subject to change.

TAKE TO THE WATER

Here are more ways to enjoy Washington's waterways:

Capitol River Cruises
800-405-5511
www.capitolrivercruises.com

Key Bridge Boathouse
3500 Water St., NW, Washington, DC 20007
202-337-9642
www.boatingindc.com

Odyssey Washington
600 Water St., SW, Washington, DC 20024
866-306-2469
www.odysseycruises.com/washington-dc
Metro: Waterfront-SEU (Green Line)

Potomac Riverboat Company
Washington Harbour, Georgetown
31st & K Sts., NW, Washington, DC 20007
877-511-2528
www.potomacriverboatco.com

Tidal Basin Paddle Boats
1501 Maine Ave., SW, Washington, DC 20024
202-479-2426
www.tidalbasinpaddleboats.com

TOUR THE ONLY MUSEUM
DEDICATED TO WOMEN IN THE ARTS

You'll know the National Museum of Women in the Arts when you see the sculptures on the island in front of a giftbox-like building. Inside, you'll find 4,500 pieces of art by more than 1,000 female artists, from the sixteenth century to the present.

The museum is the only one in the world dedicated to women in the arts. Notable exhibits include botanical prints by Maria Sibylla, paintings by Elisabetta Sirani, sculptures by Sarah Bernhardt, drawings by Mary Cassatt, photographs by Louise Dahl-Wolfe, and videos by Dara Birnbaum, just to name a few.

The museum hosts concerts, workshops, frequent gallery talks, and a monthly community day when admission is free. It also hosts exhibit preview days for members.

National Museum of Women in the Arts
1250 New York Ave., NW, Washington, DC 20005
202-783-5000
www.nmwa.org
Metro: Metro Center (Red, Blue, Silver, Orange lines)

TRAVEL THE WORLD
ON THE PASSPORT DC EMBASSY TOUR

Mark your calendar for May and travel the world in one month during the Passport DC Embassy Tour, a celebration of the world embassies located in DC. Activities include the Around the World Embassy Tour, the European Embassies Open House, and the Fiesta Asia Street Festival. Each event is held on a separate Saturday.

Grab your free souvenir passport from the Passport DC kiosks and get ready to experience the food and culture of seventy countries across six continents in one day. Start your journey on International Drive, where lines are shorter. Don't miss the echo chamber at the Canadian embassy rotunda, the Ippakutei Tea House at the Japanese embassy, the pubs at the British and Irish embassies, and the sauna at the Finnish embassy.

Passport DC Embassy Tour
www.culturaltourismdc.org/portal/passport-dc1
Metro: Dupont Circle and Van Ness (Red Line)
See also: Walk the Neighborhood Heritage Trails on page 60.

VISIT
PRESIDENT WILSON'S HOUSE

Ever wonder what life is like after the presidency? At the President Woodrow Wilson House, you can experience the twenty-eighth president's daily life post-White House.

The house on S Street is where Wilson resided from the end of his presidency in 1921 until his death in 1924. His wife resided there until her death in 1961, at which point the home became a monument to President Wilson.

Step inside and explore the study, the solarium, and the drawing room (with a Steinway piano as its focal piece). Then explore the formal gardens that extend beyond the solarium.

You can also play vintage games from the 1920s to the 1940s at the museum during its monthly game night, an after-hours, midweek happy hour.

The President Woodrow Wilson House
2340 S St., NW, Washington, DC 20008
202-387-4062
www.woodrowwilsonhouse.org
Metro: Dupont Circle (Red Line)

VIEW
THE FOUNDING DOCUMENTS

Inside the Rotunda for the Charters of Freedom at the National Archives are the documents this country was built on: the Declaration of Independence, which separated the thirteen colonies from Great Britain, the Constitution of the United States, and the Bill of Rights.

You can go "behind-the-walls" of the Rotunda with a tour of the public vaults, a permanent interactive exhibit that takes you through the stacks and vaults of the archives. The tour begins in the Record of America and features letters written by George Washington, telegrams from Abraham Lincoln, the 1823 copper plate of the Declaration of Independence, and a facsimile of the Emancipation Proclamation. The exhibit includes five additional vaults, each reflecting a theme from the Constitution.

National Archives
700 Pennsylvania Ave., NW, Washington, DC 20408
202-357-5000
www.archives.gov
Metro: Archives-Navy Memorial (Yellow, Green lines)

Skip the line. Get your tickets before you go. It's worth the $1.50 convenience fee.

VISIT
1600 PENNSYLVANIA AVENUE

Go behind the gates at 1600 Pennsylvania Avenue and see the People's House from the inside. Self-guided tours are available—by advance request only—Tuesday through Thursday mornings, and Fridays and Saturdays through the lunch hour.

The thirty-minute tour takes you to the library, the Vermeil Room, the China Room, and the East Garden Room on the ground floor, and the Cross Hall, East Room, Green Room, Blue Room, Red Room, and State Dining Room on the second floor.

Be sure to look out the window in the Blue Room. The view of the Washington Monument is one-of-a-kind.

White House
1600 Pennsylvania Ave., NW, Washington, DC 20500
202-456-7041
www.whitehouse.gov/about/tours-and-events
Metro: Federal Triangle, McPherson Square (Blue, Silver, Orange lines),
Metro Center (Red, Blue, Silver, Orange lines)

WHITE HOUSE VISIT TIPS

Submit your tour request to your senator or congressional representative at least twenty-one days in advance. Advance requests—up to six months—are highly recommended.

Arrive at least fifteen minutes early to allow for screening and check-in. And leave all your belongings at your hotel or in your car. The only thing you can carry in is your government-issued photo ID (phones are okay, but you won't be allowed to use them). Families, especially ones with small children, should visit a restroom before checking in.

Call the twenty-four-hour information line before you go. The White House is subject to closures.

• •

MARK YOUR CALENDAR FOR THESE SPRING EVENTS

White House Spring Garden Tour

For one weekend in April, the White House opens its gardens to visitors. The tour includes the Jacqueline Kennedy Garden, the Rose Garden, the South Lawn, and the White House Kitchen Garden. The same-day tickets are first-come, first-serve and are distributed by the National Park Service. Dates are announced on the White House website in early spring.

White House Easter Egg Roll

This family favorite is held on the Monday after Easter. Tickets are available by lottery only, which opens early in the year at www.recreation.gov.

UNLOCK THE SECRET
DOORS AT THE O STREET MUSEUM

Inside an elegant Dupont Circle townhome is a one-of-a-kind museum that explores and celebrates multiple kinds of art.

Immerse yourself in the creative process when you tour the O Street Museum. Create your own adventure as you go on a treasure hunt through more than sixty rooms, looking for secret doors, jeweled guitars, books, and more. For a few extra dollars, you can upgrade your adventure to include champagne, a numerology chart, or a tour of the ultra-private penthouse suite.

Tours must be reserved online. Tickets are not available at the door. The museum is open every day from 11 a.m. to 4 p.m., and exhibits change daily.

Experience the museum anew with every visit.

O Street Museum
2020 O St., NW, Washington, DC 20036
202-496-2000
www.omuseum.org
Metro: Dupont Circle (Red Line)

The O Street Museum is located at the Mansion on O Street. The mansion is open to the public on Sundays for brunch and tea, and Mondays for lunch and happy hour.

TAKE A TOUR
OF TUDOR PLACE

Ever wonder what George Washington penned to his wife, Martha? At Tudor Place, you can view one of only three letters archived from the first president of the United States, along with the largest collection from the first couple this side of the Potomac. The collection features 5,000 books and a number of personal items.

In all, Tudor Place is home to more than 15,000 artifacts from the mid-eighteenth to twentieth century, which you can see on any number of tours offered by the museum. Explore Tudor Place during a seasonal tour, like the half-priced "A Visit with Presidents" in February and March; the garden tour April through August; or on a jaunt, like the behind-the-scenes tour and the Downton Abbey tour. You can even stay for tea to complete the experience.

Tudor Place Historic House & Garden
1644 31st St., NW, Washington, DC 20007
202-965-0400
www.tudorplace.org
Metro: Foggy Bottom (Blue, Silver, Orange lines); transfer to Metrobus

VISIT THE PHILLIPS
AFTER 5 p.m.

On the first Thursday of the month, the Phillips Collection is open extended hours, from 5-8:30 p.m., for Phillips After 5, an evening of art, music, food, drinks, and gallery talks. Reservations are highly recommended as this popular event sells out.

Phillips After 5 is just one of many events held at the Phillips Collection. Other notable happenings include Conversations With Artists and the Sunday Concert Series.

The Phillips Collection was the country's first museum of modern art. Today, it features both modern and contemporary art and is filled with impressionistic paintings. The museum hosts special exhibitions and rearranges its permanent exhibits frequently, creating a new experience with every visit. Additionally, there are self-guided tours that can be downloaded from the museum's website to enhance the experience. If you're exploring the museum with kids, download the Discovery Pack before you go.

The Phillips Collection
1600 21st St., NW, Washington, DC 20009
202-387-2151
www.phillipscollection.org
Metro: Dupont Circle (Red Line)

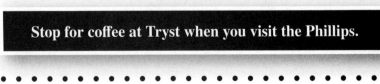

Stop for coffee at Tryst when you visit the Phillips.

● ●

VOLUNTEER
AT THE MEMORIAL DAY PARADE

Celebrate Memorial Day at the National Memorial Day Parade. Held the afternoon of Memorial Day to commemorate those who have served and sacrificed, the parade begins at 7th Street on the National Mall and travels west on Constitution Avenue, ending at 17th Street.

The parade passes by the Washington Monument, the White House, numerous museums, and thousands of spectators, and it features floats, marching bands, service groups, celebrities, and, of course, veterans.

You can participate, too, by volunteering. Helpers are needed to assemble and disperse the parade participants and guide them along the route. It's a behind-the-scenes chance to be a part of the largest Memorial Day event in the country, and an opportunity to personally thank servicemen, an experience you won't soon forget.

National Memorial Day Parade
Constitution Ave. between 7th and 17th Sts.
www.americanveteranscenter.org/parade
Metro: Archives-Navy Memorial (Yellow, Green lines)

Make it an overnight. See the Rolling Thunder motorcycle run and the National Memorial Day concert the day before. www.rollingthunderrun.com www.pbs.org/national-memorial-day-concert

VISIT
THE WORLD'S LARGEST LIBRARY

This is not your average library. The Library of Congress is the world's largest, with a collection that exceeds 158 million items. It's more than a resource for Congress, it's a resource for all.

Explore the library by first taking a tour of the Jefferson Building. The free one-hour self-guided walking tour tells the story of the library and its collections. You'll see both the Great Hall and the Main Reading Room from above.

Docent-guided tours are also available and organized by theme. Check the public tour schedule before you go.

If you're visiting with kids during peak times, take the family tour of the library instead. Then stop in the Young Readers Center for story time.

Library of Congress
10 First St., SE, Washington, DC 20540
202-707-9779
www.loc.gov
Metro: Capitol South (Blue, Silver, Orange lines),
Union Station (Red Line)

LIBRARY TIP

If you are conducting research and are over age sixteen, you can visit the Main Reading Room rather than just see it from above. All you need is a Reader Identification Card, available from the Reader Registration Station in the Madison Building.

• •

GET YOUR BOOK ON

Mark your calendar for the Library of Congress' annual National Book Festival, held at the end of August, and plan to visit these bookish destinations, too:

Kramerbooks & Afterwords Cafe
1517 Connecticut Ave., NW, Washington, DC 20036
202-387-1400
www.kramers.com
Metro: Dupont Circle (Red Line)

Martin Luther King Jr. Memorial Library
901 G St., NW, Washington, DC 20001
202-727-0321
www.dclibrary.org
Metro: Gallery Place-Chinatown (Red, Yellow, Green lines)

Politics and Prose
5015 Connecticut Ave., NW, Washington, DC 20008
202-364-1919
www.politics-prose.com
Metro: Tenleytown-AU (Red Line)

WALK THE HALLS
OF CEDAR HILL

Hear the story of Frederick Douglass as you tour the Washington, DC, house he called home from 1878 until his death in 1895. The house sits atop Cedar Hill, overlooking the city.

The tour begins at the Visitor Center, then ascends eighty-five steps to the house (there's also a ramp) and its columned front porch. The tour covers seven rooms on the first floor, including the library where Douglass wrote, and six bedrooms on the second floor, among them the room where Douglass slept.

Tickets are required to tour the house and must be purchased in advance. The fee is nominal. It is free, however, to tour the Visitor Center and the grounds. The Visitor Center features exhibits, a bookstore, and a movie about Douglass' life.

Frederick Douglass National Historic Site
1411 W St., SE, Washington, DC 20020
202-426-5961
www.nps.gov/frdo/index.htm
Metro: Anacostia (Green Line); transfer to the B2 bus to Mt. Ranier

---

The property offers one of the best views of Washington, DC. Soak in the scenery while you enjoy a picnic on the grounds.

MAKE A DAY OF IT

While you're in Anacostia, take some time to notice the varied architecture of the frame houses and tour the Anacostia Community Museum. On summer weekends, get to the museum and the Frederick Douglass National Historic Site by taking the free Shuttle Anacostia from the National Mall. The Frederick Douglass house borders the east side of the Anacostia Historic District.

Anacostia Historic District
Twenty blocks between Martin Luther King Avenue, Good Hope Road, Fendall Street, Bangor Street, and Morris Road.
www.nps.gov/nr/travel/wash/dc90.htm

Anacostia Community Museum
1901 Fort Place, SE, Washington, DC 20020
202-633-4820
www.anacostia.si.edu

WITNESS AN ORAL ARGUMENT
AT THE SUPREME COURT

See the country's highest court in action. The Supreme Court justices hear oral arguments from October to May. The sessions are held in two-week intervals on Mondays, Tuesdays, and Wednesdays at 10 and 11a.m.

Sessions are open to the public, but seating is limited, so arrive early to queue up. Seating begins at 9:30 a.m. for those wishing to attend the entire session and at 10 a.m. for those waiting in the express line, content with a brief, three-minute visit inside the courtroom.

If you miss the oral arguments, check out the Courtroom Lectures instead. These are held every hour on the half-hour from 9:30 a.m. to 3:30 p.m. when the court is not in session.

Supreme Court of the United States
1 First St., NE, Washington, DC 20543
202-479-3030
www.supremecourt.gov
Metro: Capitol South (Blue, Silver, Orange lines), Union Station (Red Line)

TIP

After your visit, head over to the Monocle
for lunch. You may find yourself dining
beside the justices and rubbing elbows with
politicians. Order the crab cakes.

The Monocle Restaurant
107 D St., NE, Washington, DC 20002
202-546-4488
www.themonocle.com
Metro: Capitol South (Blue, Silver, Orange lines),
Union Station (Red Line)

SUGGESTED ITINERARIES

ALL THE PRESIDENT'S MEN

ALL THE WORLD'S A STAGE

FUN FOR THE FAMILY

HISTORIC HOUSES AND GARDENS

OF MONUMENTS AND MEMORIALS

• •

• •

ACTIVITIES BY SEASON

DC is an all-seasons destination, but some activities are season-specific or best visited during a particular time of year.

SPRING

SUMMER

FALL

WINTER

• •

EVENTS BY MONTH

JANUARY
DC Restaurant Week, 17
Martin Luther King Jr. Day
 of Service, 94

FEBRUARY
Atlas Intersections Festival, 43
Chinese New Year Festival, 20
Date Night DC, 30
Washington DC International
 Film Festival, 39

MARCH
DC Environmental Film Fest, 39
National Cherry Blossom
 Festival, 67
Orchard Month at Hillwood
 Estates, 107
Rock 'n' Roll DC Marathon, 72

APRIL
Cherry Blossom Ten-Miler, 67
Easter Monday at the Zoo, 49
Shakespeare's Birthday
 Celebration, 114
Smithsonian Craft Show, 51

MAY
Memorial Day Weekend Concert
 and Parade, 131
National Police Week, 84
Passport DC, 123
Post Hunt, 69
Rolling Thunder, 131

JUNE
DC Jazz Festival, 35
National Capital Barbecue Battle, 3
Smithsonian Folklife Festival, 51

JULY
Animals in the Sky, 49
Brew at the Zoo, 49
Capital Fringe Festival, 88

AUGUST
Bao Bao's Birthday, 49
DC Beer Week, 17
DC Restaurant Week, 17
National Book Festival, 133

SEPTEMBER
50 States & 13 Colonies Ride, 58
Boundary Stones Bike Ride, 59
Crafty Bastards Arts & Crafts
 Fair, 28
DC Shorts Film Festival, 39
H Street Festival, 46
Rock 'n' Roar, 49
Zoo Fiesta, 49

OCTOBER
17th Street High Heel Race, 33
Autumn Conservation Festival, 49
Boo at the Zoo, 49
Fall Fest at Lincoln's Cottage, 112
Marine Corps Marathon, 53
Night of the Living Zoo, 49

NOVEMBER
Holiday Ice Skating, 64
Reel Affirmations, 39

DECEMBER
Downtown Holiday Market, 44
National Chanukah Menorah
 Lighting on the Ellipse, 44
National Christmas Tree Lighting, 44
ZooLights, 44

• •

INDEX

142

• •

143

● ●